THE
LITTLE FLOWER

ST. THÉRÈSE OF LISIEUX

THE
IRISH CONNECTION

COLM KEANE & UNA O'HAGAN

CAPEL
ISLAND

First published in Ireland in 2018

by

CAPEL ISLAND PRESS
Baile na nGall,
Ring, Dungarvan,
County Waterford,
Ireland

ISBN 978-1-9995920-0-4

Printed and bound by Clays Ltd, Elcograf S.p.A
Typesetting and cover design by Typeform Ltd.

For Seán

Colm Keane has published 27 books, including seven number one bestsellers, among them *Padre Pio: Irish Encounters with the Saint*, *Padre Pio: The Scent of Roses*, *Going Home*, *We'll Meet Again* and *Heading for the Light*. He is a graduate of Trinity College, Dublin, and Georgetown University, Washington DC. As a broadcaster, he won a Jacob's Award and a Glaxo Fellowship for European Science Writers.

Una O'Hagan is a former newsreader with Radio Telefís Éireann. A journalism graduate, she has interviewed Nelson Mandela, accompanied President Mary Robinson on a state visit to Australia and hosted live programmes on the deaths of former Taoisigh Jack Lynch and Garret FitzGerald and the state visit of Queen Elizabeth II to Ireland. This is her second book.

CONTENTS

1. INTRODUCTION   1

2. A KIND AND GENTLE SOUL   9

3. A SOUL TAKES FLIGHT   51

4. THE ANGEL OF THE TRENCHES   85

5. SOARING ON EAGLES WINGS   112

6. A MODERN-DAY SAINT   156

7. ACKNOWLEDGEMENTS   206

After my death I will let fall a shower of roses.

Thérèse of Lisieux

INTRODUCTION

In April 2001, a woman from County Wicklow seriously damaged her leg. Having torn and twisted her ligaments, the pain was intense, the bruising severe, and the skin was turning black. She was unable to work. The hospital strapped her leg, put her on crutches, and warned her to remain at home with her leg elevated for a minimum of six weeks.

"The pain was unbearable," Chris remarked. "My leg was killing me. I was on painkillers. It was the time St. Thérèse's relics were here. A man I knew said, 'I'm going to Gorey to visit the relics.' I said, 'Would you ask St. Thérèse to make my leg better? I have to work and I can't stay off my leg for six weeks.' He said, 'I will, of course.' And he did."

The next morning, when Chris woke up, her problem was gone. "I jumped out of the bed and onto the floor," she recalled. "I never used the crutches again. I just covered my leg up so that no one would see it and I went back to work. When I returned to the hospital, they said my leg was fine. I have no doubt it was St. Thérèse. These things don't just happen. There are no coincidences. I have no doubt it was her."

Shortly before her death, Thérèse promised to let fall from heaven a "shower of roses." These were the miracles, blessings and graces she wished to bring to those she left behind. She loved roses, observing them blossoming and blooming outside her window as she lay dying. She adored them so much that she chose them as a symbol of the multitude of revivals she promised to bring about after her death.

Thérèse's miracles have not only been numerous but diverse. Many involve cures from serious illnesses and diseases including cancer, heart failure, meningitis, septicaemia, tuberculosis and chronic arthritis. Others are spiritually affirming, offering inner peace. Some concern religious conversions. More are of a practical nature – a Dublin nun told us: "Whenever I need parking, I ask St. Thérèse. She never fails me!"

Given her extraordinary powers, it was no surprise that within a decade and a half of her death, Irish people were flocking to the French region of Normandy where she had lived and died. They travelled to get to know her, understand her, find inner calm or secure miraculous cures. Taoiseach Éamon de Valera, who became a devotee, paid a visit in the hope of restoring his failing eyesight.

Back home in Ireland, veneration grew exponentially. There was hardly a church that didn't feature a Thérèse statue. They still do so to this day. "I love looking at her statue," Kathleen, from County Kildare, says. "There is a sort of innocence about her. She is lovely. She has a very kind face. It makes me want to pray to her. I light my candle and I say my prayers. I always ask her for favours. Somehow, when you look up at her you know that she hears what you say."

Irish churches, schools, community halls and nursing homes were soon being named after the future saint. As far back as 1951, a columnist in the long-disappeared newspaper, *The Catholic Standard*, remarked on how commonplace "St. Thérèse" and "Lisieux" had become on Irish gates and front doors. They featured along with "St. Anthony", "St. Bernadette", "Lourdes", "Stella Maris" and "Prague". There even was a "Nazareth" – a clever choice "except for the difficulty of living up to it!" the writer drily remarked.

Newspapers, magazines and journals featured stories concerning Thérèse. They printed comments made by her sisters, all four of them nuns. Pauline – known as Mother Agnès, who was prioress at the Carmelite monastery in Lisieux – wrote hoping that Ireland would be saved from the horrors of war. Another sister, Céline, sent a message of support to a project in Limerick. With exposure like this, the Little Flower soon attained iconic status in Ireland. It wasn't long before she was vying with Padre Pio as the country's favourite saint.

Probably the main reason Irish people grew to love Thérèse was that she was a likeable person. "There lived some short time ago, in France, a generous and loving soul," was how Wexford cleric, Canon John Lennon, introduced her as far back as 1912. He certainly had a point. One would be hard-pressed to find someone more kind-hearted, unselfish, charming or affectionate than the Little Flower.

Thérèse Martin had a sunny disposition from the day she was born. She came into this world on 2 January 1873, in the town of Alençon, Normandy. Her mother, Zélie, was an accomplished lacemaker. Her father, Louis, was a watchmaker. They had nine children, although only five survived infancy. The last of the children – Thérèse – was the undoubted pet of the family. "She is a child who delights us all," her mother remarked.

As a baby, Thérèse came close to death, forcing her parents to place her under the care of a nearby wet nurse. Within a year, she had recovered and returned home. The family of seven – two parents and five daughters – became a tight-knit unit, full of fun and adventure, lovers of nature, talented at music and proficient at art. The credit, Thérèse later said, was all down to her parents whose "good example" she "naturally wished to follow."

The Martin family were God-loving and great practitioners of their faith. They diligently attended Mass and devotions, went to confession, and prayed with conviction. The atmosphere at home was intensely religious. The four eldest girls went on to become nuns – Marie, Pauline and Céline joined the Carmelites in Lisieux; Léonie joined the Visitation Sisters in Caen. Even as a two-year-old, Thérèse decided that she, too, would become a nun. She never changed her mind.

Following her mother's death, when Thérèse was four years old, the family left Alençon for Lisieux, located 50 miles away. After moving into their new home, Les Buissonnets, Thérèse dedicated the next decade of her life to becoming a nun. She wished to enter the local Carmelite monastery. After applying herself to the task – including making an appeal to the pope – she achieved her goal at the remarkably young age of 15.

Thérèse's time in the Lisieux Carmel was silent and solitary. Her life was dedicated to prayer, contemplation and work. Even in the few hours when conversation was permitted, the use of idle words was forbidden. A hush enveloped the convent. The chapel was eerily quiet. "The silence was so great that the slight sound made by the flickering sanctuary lamp seemed almost loud in the stillness," an Irish visitor remarked in 1913.

She suffered the deprivations of convent life without complaint, while scrupulously obeying the rules. The petty restrictions, the rigour, the discipline and the harsh conditions were endured with humility and grace. She once recalled: "I was working in the laundry, and the sister opposite, while washing handkerchiefs, repeatedly splashed me with dirty water. My first impulse was to draw back and wipe my face, to show the offender I should be glad if she would behave more quietly." Instead, Thérèse did nothing and welcomed the event.

All that time, the Little Flower remained wonderfully human, aware of her limitations and imperfections. The demands she faced were sometimes beyond her. She found it hard to concentrate during meditation. She would fall asleep while praying or during choir exercises. She even admitted: "I have not the courage to look through books for beautiful prayers. I only get a headache because of their number."

Out of all this came an extraordinarily simple, yet profound, set of insights that transformed religious thinking overnight. Great deeds, she said, are beyond most of us. Little deeds are what we do, instead. If you can't be perfect, you can at least do your best and practice all the little things you do with love. Just do them well, and offer them up to God. This she described as her little way.

Ordinary people suddenly became important. "Holiness" was instantly within their grasp. They no longer needed to perform heroic acts, or accomplish great deeds, to become saints. "It is enough," she said, "to acknowledge our nothingness, and like children surrender ourselves into the arms of the good God." We are all equal in that task, she added: "As the sun shines both on the cedar and on the floweret, so the Divine Son illuminates every soul, great and small."

The first steps towards chronicling Thérèse's little way were taken between the end of 1894 and the start of 1895, when she was around 22 years old. A vivacious talker and a good mimic, she was asked to tell stories from her childhood to her fellow sisters in the Carmel. Having done so, to great effect, two of her sisters – Marie and Pauline – felt it might be a good idea to write the stories down. Pauline, who was the Carmel's prioress at the time, instructed Thérèse to do so.

The project might have ended there but for the unfortunate arrival of tuberculosis (TB) into Thérèse's life in the spring of 1896. The insidious bacterium, mycobacterium tuberculosis, invaded Thérèse's lungs and effectively crippled her life. While ill, she wrote further accounts of her time growing up and as a nun in the Carmel. She also described her little way. She stopped writing three months before she died. The pencil fell from her hand as she wrote the last word – love.

It was only after Thérèse's death that the manuscripts first saw the light of day. Initially published for distribution to the Carmelite convents of France, the book soon took off. A first run of 2,000 copies, including surplus copies for public sale, disappeared quickly. Soon there was a second run, of 4,000 copies. Then there was another run, and then another and another. The 24-year-old's autobiography, with an initial working title of *A Love Song or Passage of an Angel* but later called *Story of a Soul*, was on its way.

The book had a revolutionary impact following its release. Its core message was not only simple and understandable, but millions of miles removed from the incomprehensible ecclesiastical expositions that had been written before. It challenged a Church that had become grandiose and pompous, with its ostentatious wealth, bishops' palaces and sartorial elegance including ornate vestments and stoles threaded in silver and gold. Ordinary Catholics – and non-Catholics, too – rediscovered their beliefs.

The book became an international runaway success. First generation Irish-American, Cardinal Dennis Dougherty, explained that when passing through China in 1916 he was given a copy of the autobiography translated into Chinese. A few weeks later, in Tokyo, a Japanese Jesuit presented him with a copy translated into Japanese. A short time afterwards, he was in Arabia and was presented with three copies in Arabic. Apart from the Bible, no other book could match that sort of world-wide appeal.

The only sadness was that, by the time of its release, the book's author was missing. Her life on earth had come to a close in the autumn of 1897. Her final battle with TB had been a tough one and she had known the end was near. One evening, while lying in bed, she had welcomed her sister, Pauline, with joy. "Mother," she said, "some notes from a concert far away have just reached my ears, and have made me think that soon I shall be listening to the wondrous melodies of paradise." She didn't have long to wait.

Thérèse died on 30 September 1897, aged 24. Her sister Pauline described how, towards the end, there was a strange commotion by the window: "A multitude of little birds took their station on a tree beside the wide open window of the infirmary, where they continued to sing with all their might until her death." Never before had the garden witnessed such a concert.

"I was rather depressed by the contrast between so much suffering within and the joyous notes without," Thérèse's sister reflected. Although that Thursday in September 1897 had been generally dark and rainy, nevertheless, towards seven o'clock in the evening, the clouds dispersed with unusual speed. "Soon the stars were shining in a bright, clear sky," Pauline noted. Somewhere up there, among those stars, the Little Flower was on her way to heaven.

A KIND AND
GENTLE SOUL

Thérèse of Lisieux was tall by the standards of her day. She was not only the tallest in her family but, at 5ft 4in, she was close to the height of most men in France. It didn't greatly please her. When questioned by her sister Céline, she replied: "I should prefer to be short in order to be *little* in every way."

Thérèse loved everything that was little. God loved little children, she remarked. "To him that is little, mercy is granted," she noted. She also loved the little flowers in the fields. Not every flower could be great, she observed – even the lesser ones, like the daisies and violets, were beloved by God.

Not surprisingly, Thérèse referred to herself as the Little Flower. She also devised a path to heaven called her little way – "very short and very straight, a little way that is wholly new." Although her time on earth was short, what she achieved from birth to death was far from little, as we are about to see.

A wet nurse, Rose Taillé, saved Thérèse's life shortly after her birth. The practise of wet nursing babies was common in France and Ireland at the time.

At thirty minutes before midnight, on 2 January 1873, a baby girl was born to Zélie Martin in the town of Alençon, France. The mother had many reasons to be happy. Four of her previous children had died as infants, but this baby seemed fine. Aged 41, she had feared the worst. Matters were further complicated by a tumour in her breast and an inability to properly breastfeed her babies.

Nothing could match Zélie's motherly joy as she looked at her beautiful child. The following day, she wrote to her sister-in-law: "My little daughter was born yesterday, Thursday, at 11.30 at night. She is very strong and very well; they tell me she weighs eight pounds. Let us put it at six; that is already not bad. She seems to be very pretty." Although expecting and hoping to deliver a boy, the new arrival made her "very happy," she said.

Two months later, a panic-stricken Zélie was desperately battling to save her child's life. The little girl's health had faded rapidly. She wasn't sleeping; her bowels were inflamed; death seemed a matter of days away. Her doctor advised that, without the help of a wet nurse, little Marie Françoise Thérèse Martin had no hope of survival. Zélie's motherly instincts kicked in and she decided to take action.

One morning, at dawn, she set out on a seven-mile walk to the nearby commune of Semallé. Zélie undertook the journey alone, as her husband was away from home. She was heading to Rose Taillé, a small farmer's wife, aged 37, who had previously breastfed two of her sons. The fact that both sons had died, despite the care they were given, was a measure of Zélie's desperation that day. Her mind must have been in turmoil as she walked along.

Despite having four sons of her own – the youngest just a year old – Rose agreed to return with Zélie to Alençon. She was horrified by what she saw there. Thérèse looked frail and weak, and was clearly at the edge of death. She immediately set about breastfeeding the child. Zélie prayed to St. Joseph upstairs.

"I went quickly up to my room," Zélie later wrote, "and knelt at the feet of Saint Joseph, asking him for the favour of curing the little one, while resigning myself to God's will if He wanted to take the child. I do not cry often, but my tears flowed when I was saying this prayer. I did not know if I should go down, but I decided to do so. And what did I see? The child was sucking wholeheartedly, and did not give up until one o'clock in the afternoon. Then she threw up a few mouthfuls and fell back on the wet nurse as though she were dead."

Zélie's blood turned to ice. Another woman, who was present, started weeping. They were sure Thérèse had died. "She was so calm, so peaceful, that I thanked God for having had her die so easily," the crestfallen mother recalled. They bent over the baby trying to find some sign of life. Suddenly, Thérèse opened her eyes, looked up, and smiled!

For the next year, Thérèse lived with Rose Taillé at her modest home in Semallé. By allowing her to do so, Zélie was merely reflecting a practise that was widespread in France – using a wet nurse to nourish a child. Urban mothers, from noble or wealthy families, frequently sent their babies to the countryside to be nursed by peasant women. Poorer working mothers did the same, enabling them to earn much-needed money. At one stage, Paris seemed empty of babies, so many were farmed out for rural wet nursing.

The tradition in Ireland was similar. A nineteenth-century British study noted that Dublin hospitals sent babies to rural wet nurses and assessed their progress once a year. The nurses were paid £3 annually for feeding and clothing the infants in their care. Wealthy families organised their own live-in wet nurses. In Boston the majority of documented wet nurses were Irish.

In those pre-baby food days, Zélie Martin was merely doing what many women did at the time.

Thérèse thrived in the care of Rose, who became in effect her surrogate mother. Smothered with love and affection, she developed into a happy, healthy, watchful young child. Rose loved her "little flower", placing her on a wheelbarrow and bringing her into the fields while she worked. Thérèse loved it. Soon, she had grown accustomed to country ways, adoring flowers and all the beauties of nature.

Zélie met Thérèse often, either visiting her in Semallé or meeting her when Rose came to sell farm produce at the market in town. She noted how, on market days, her little Thérèse would cling to Rose just like a scared child would cling to its mother. She screamed when Zélie's acquaintances, dressed in their finery and exotic hats, would lift her up. They would quickly return Thérèse to the arms of her beloved Rose at her market stall, where she would quieten down.

When Thérèse visited her family home, she also felt out of place. In a letter, Zélie described how, one Sunday, Rose arrived with her four sons to attend Mass in town. She passed the child on to the Martins before heading for church. "The little one didn't want that at all, and she cried uncontrollably!" she explained. Rose had to be recalled in the middle of Mass. Thérèse was "instantly consoled," Zélie remarked.

There are some inferences to be drawn from the relationship between Thérèse and Rose, her wet nurse. It was through Rose that Thérèse first developed her love of all things "ordinary", prompting her, later on, to reject the trappings of privilege and develop her little way. It was also through Rose – and eventually through Zélie – that Thérèse learned the meaning of love; a love that would later become her intense love of God. Finally, it was through Rose that she learned to love nature – especially flowers.

Flowers were central to the young life of Thérèse of Lisieux. Like many Irish people, she loved them. She believed they were the key to understanding God's creation.

While travelling through Normandy, in 1914, an Irish pilgrim was overwhelmed by the splendour of the countryside. Normandy, he said, was a place of prosperous-looking villages nestled in fat valleys. Everywhere there was beauty – "beauty of verdure, of refinement, of colour." The orchards, farmhouses and chateaux seemed to be asleep in the sunshine. The land laughed with plenty.

The Irish visitor particularly noted the plants and flowers around Lisieux. Violets, primroses and hyacinths blossomed on the roadsides. "In the dark umbrageous woods the brown-topped orchid bloomed," Rev. J. A. Dowling remarked. The hedgerows were veiled in a tender shade of green. You could almost see the sun at work softening sheath and leaf and bud.

This was the countryside which Thérèse had loved so much. Poppies, irises and dahlias, coloured red, blue-purple and pink, were everywhere to be seen. Fields of yellow sunflowers bent under the summer sun. Lilacs, roses and tulips decorated people's homes. Window boxes dripped with geraniums and petunias. Monet and Fantin-Latour lived not far away – the former painting dreamy ponds of water lilies; the latter painting multicoloured flowers in vases.

Thérèse adored flowers. As a child, in Alençon, she loved being taken by her father and mother for her Sunday walks in the countryside, where she could admire the flowers in the fields.

She later explained how, on those early walks, the cornflowers, poppies and marguerites impressed themselves on her childish heart and lifted her soul to heaven. She loved them just as fondly after moving to Lisieux, where, significantly, the Martins called their home Les Buissonnets or "The Little Bushes".

Thérèse particularly liked the simple wild flowers that no one noticed. They were just like her, she thought – small and unassuming, seemingly insignificant, yet as important as the great flowers in the eyes of the God who created them. She would pick them in the fields and bring them home. Early on, she would worry that picking the flowers might hurt them, and she would ask her sister Céline if they would be alright.

When Thérèse entered the Carmel, she feared she would never see her beloved flowers again. It didn't work out like that. Bouquets arrived in abundance, sent from the world outside, their purpose being to decorate the altar. All her best-loved flowers were there – the cornflowers, poppies and marguerites – but one was missing, the humble, common wildflower called the purple vetch. Then, one day, there it was. Her "little friend" had joined her, gladdening her young heart.

Perhaps it was no surprise, then, that flowers dominated Thérèse's thoughts and, later, her legend – she did, after all, become known as the Little Flower and her promised "shower of roses" brought many blessings and cures. She also reserved for her beautiful cornflowers, daisies, violets, lilies, forget-me-nots and roses a central place in *Story of a Soul*.

How, she wondered, did all souls not receive the same amount of grace? How could great sinners like St. Augustine and St. Paul be so loved in the eyes of God? How could so many others – good people who had never heard of Him – be lost?

How were we all so different? Why did it all seem so unequal and so unfair?

She found the answer in flowers. Every flower is beautiful, she argued. The brilliance of the rose and the whiteness of the lily are no more important than the perfume of the violet or the sweet simplicity of the daisy. If all the lowly flowers were roses, the fields would no longer be "enamelled with lovely hues" and nature would lose its springtime beauty. In short, even the simple field flower charms God.

It is the same with souls, she said. The saints may be the lilies or the roses, but there are lesser people – like the daisies or the violets – who play an equal role. They, too, sit at His feet, part of the great scheme of things. Just like the saints, their role is to gladden God. The more gladly they do it the greater is their perfection.

It was no coincidence that a simple flower also played a central role in one of the most poignant moments in Thérèse's life. It was the day she informed her father of her intention to become a nun. The location was the garden of the family home. It was towards evening. The sun's rays shone over the tops of the trees and the birds were singing their goodnight prayers. Her father sat there, absorbed by the wonders that surrounded him, his face a picture of peace.

Thérèse approached him, her eyes full of tears. He held her close and then rose from his seat. Together they slowly walked up and down the garden. Still sobbing, Thérèse told him she wished to enter the Carmel. Although she was only 14 and a half, she explained that she hoped to do so soon. Fighting back his tears, her father eventually gave his blessing.

That wonderful summer's evening, before leaving the garden, her father pointed to some flowers growing in an old stone wall. He picked one and gave it to Thérèse. It was a little white flower, which he said was cared for by God who had watched over it and nourished it until it had grown to the size it was now. Thérèse knew the little flower's story was her own story, too.

She also noted that the flower still had its roots and was destined to thrive elsewhere in fertile soil. Again, she thought, it was just like her own life – she would soon leave home and move to the Carmel, where she would blossom as a Servant of God. Later, she fastened the flower to a picture of Our Lady of Victories and kept it for the remainder of her days. In time, the stalk broke, close to the root, but by then she was dying. That parallel wasn't lost on Thérèse, either. She knew there was a lot to be learned from flowers.

Thérèse's early childhood was spent with her family in Alençon. Those were the happiest years of her life.

Sligo-born Fr. William Michael Cunningham, who wrote a book on Thérèse in 1914, chose suitably accurate words to describe the Little Flower as a child. She was "impulsive, open, intelligent, and stubborn," he remarked. Drawing from his many visits to Normandy and his knowledge of the future saint, his words summed up his subject to a tee.

It would be hard to find a child who was more innocently candid, spontaneously hot-headed, razor-sharp or as stubborn as a mule as Thérèse. Her mother caught her childhood character to perfection. Writing of her "little puss" in a letter, she remarked that not only was she "heedless" and "very intelligent" but that her "stubbornness is almost unconquerable. When she has said 'no,' nothing will make her change; one could leave her all day in the cellar without getting her to say 'yes.' She would sooner sleep there."

With her blonde hair, blue eyes, chubby face and affectionate demeanour, Thérèse charmed everyone who met her. She was the favourite of the family. Her father called her his "little queen". The other girls wanted to be with her, especially the next-youngest sister, Céline. "She is a child who delights us all," her mother said.

She was so attached to her "Mamma" that she followed her wherever she went. "The dear little thing will hardly leave me, she follows me everywhere," her mother wrote. "She will not even go upstairs alone without calling me at each step, 'Mamma! Mamma!' and if I forget to answer 'Yes, darling!' she waits where she is, and will not move."

There's no doubt Thérèse was stubborn. One day, her mother tested how headstrong she was. Smiling, she said to the child: "If you will kiss the ground I will give you a halfpenny." Thérèse picks up the story: "In those days a halfpenny was a fortune, and in order to gain it I had not far to stoop, for I was so tiny there was not much distance between me and the ground; but my pride was up in arms, and holding myself very erect, I said, 'No, thank you, Mamma, I would rather go without it.'"

Her uninhibited directness would bring a smile to your face. "She is extraordinarily outspoken," her mother remarked. On one occasion, when she was four, she attended a Holy Hour and exclaimed: "It's lovelier than usual, but it's very long all the same." Another time, she ran to her mother and confessed: "Mamma, I have pushed Céline; I slapped her once, but I'll not

17

do it again." Later in life, she would candidly admit to falling asleep while praying.

She was also anxious to confess her failings. Once, having damaged a small piece of wallpaper, she couldn't wait to own up to her father. "When he came home four hours later, everyone else had forgotten about it, but she ran at once to Marie saying: 'Tell Papa that I tore the paper.' She waited there like a criminal for sentence; but she thinks she is more easily forgiven if she accuses herself," her mother recalled.

Nothing enchanted Thérèse more than the grandeur of nature. "Even at that age I loved far-stretching views, sunlit spaces and stately trees; in a word, all nature charmed me and lifted up my soul to heaven." She was particularly captivated by the sky and the sea. Living in the countryside, the stars would shimmer at night. At the nearby Normandy coast, she would witness the glories of the sea.

"I remember that I used to look up at the stars with inexpressible delight," she recalled of times spent with her father observing the night sky. "Orion's belt fascinated me especially, for I saw in it a likeness to the letter 'T'. 'Look, Papa,' I would cry, 'my name is written in heaven!'" A little later, she saw the sea for the first time. "The sight made a deep impression on me," she remembered. "I could not take my eyes off it. Its majesty, and the roar of the waves, all spoke to my soul of the greatness and power of God."

Above all, the young Thérèse practised holiness. At one stage, when too young to attend church, she would stage Sunday Mass at home. Her sister, Céline, would provide the bread, bringing it back from the chapel. "One day she had not brought

18

any – what was to be done? I could not do without it, for I called this little feast my Mass," Thérèse recollected.

"A bright idea struck me: 'You have no blessed bread! – make some.' Céline immediately opened the cupboard, took out the bread, cut a tiny bit off, and after saying a Hail Mary quite solemnly over it, triumphantly presented it to me; and I, making the Sign of the Cross, ate it with devotion, fancying it tasted exactly like the real blessed bread."

She prayed with great intensity, modelling herself on her beloved father. "I had only to look at him to know how the saints pray," she remarked. At night, her sister Pauline would put her to bed. "Have I been good today? Is God pleased with me? Will the angels watch over me?" Thérèse would ask. The answer was always "Yes."

Looking back, these first four and a half years of Thérèse's life were the most joyful she would experience in her life. "Dear Mother, how happy I was at that age," she later said. They were the "sunny years of my childhood," as she put it – a time of "loving smiles and tender caresses" and a period that, despite its shortness, was "rich in memories." Unfortunately, those days would come to an end, and the end would come all too soon.

When Thérèse was four and a half years old, her mother died from breast cancer. The death changed Thérèse's life.

The growing incidence of cancer made headline news in the late nineteenth century. Irish and French press reports referred to "the rapid increase of a much-dreaded disease." The remark was well-judged, as cancer deaths had multiplied fivefold in the previous 50 years. One in nine of all females were dying from the disease, many of them from cancer of the breast.

Quack cures abounded. One herbal remedy "proved successful in every case of cancer of the lips, tongue, nose and breast where it has been tried," its manufacturer claimed. Another product, Moonseed Bitters, guaranteed a cure for "internal and external cancers." Coroners' courts witnessed the consequences of quack cures, with one case alone, in Galway, in 1884, recording the death of a woman from a "dark powder" applied to her breast.

Like other cancer sufferers, Zélie Martin was desperate for a cure. Her worries began in 1865 when the first symptoms of the disease appeared. Her brother was a student pharmacist in Paris and she asked him for advice. For whatever reason, her requests to find a suitable specialist came to nothing. With prospects of an early surgical intervention gone, the cancer progressed and her fate was sealed.

When Zélie finally sought medical advice, the news was bad. "The doctor looked into the eyes of this calm little woman who came to be examined," according to the Earl of Wicklow in his 1961 translation of Louise André-Delastre's book *Azélie Martin: Mère de Sainte Thérèse de l'Enfant-Jésus.* "Do you know that what you have is of a very serious nature?" he asked. There wasn't a flicker of her eyes. "A fibrous tumour," she was told. As he filled in a prescription for medicine, she smiled sceptically and asked: "What would be the use?" He replied abruptly: "None."

Zélie suffered badly for the remainder of her life. Her tumour grew in size and the pain intensified. Remedies provided by her brother, who was now a pharmacist in Lisieux, had no effect. A further tumour was discovered in her neck. The conclusion of a second specialist was just as grim as the first – the time for an operation had passed; it was now the time for prayer.

Together with her three eldest children, Zélie visited Lourdes in search of a cure. It was a disastrous trip. "The invalid, missing two steps of the staircase in the hotel, gave herself such a twist in the neck that for a long time she was to ascribe to it the increase in her sufferings," the Earl's book noted. Two of her accompanying daughters lost valuable rosary beads. They even missed the train, at Angers, on their return home. Zélie ended up exhausted.

The atmosphere at home grew dark. The two youngest girls – Thérèse and Céline – were farmed out to a family friend by day and felt like "poor little exiles." Once, when they forgot to say their prayers, they told their mother, but her response surprised them. "She took us to a large room, and left us there. Céline looked at me in amazement. I was equally astonished, and exclaimed: 'This is not like Mamma, she always said our prayers with us.'" On another occasion, they wished to offer a precious apricot to their mother, but she was too unwell to eat it.

On the evening of 26 August 1877, Zélie Martin, aged 46, received Extreme Unction. The sacrament left a deep impression on Thérèse. "I can still see the place where I knelt, and hear my poor father's sobs," she wrote in *Story of a Soul*. Two days later, the atmosphere became darker still when Zélie passed away, and the life Thérèse had grown to know and love became no more.

Thérèse learned of her mother's death on the morning of 29 August. She reacted with shock and sadness. Her senses were numbed and her mind bewildered. Aged just four and a half, she kept her thoughts to herself. Not only had she lost her "second" mother – the first being her wet nurse Rose Taillé – but she was now confronted with death and the sadness that stretched ahead.

"My father took me in his arms and said: 'Come and kiss your dear mother for the last time,'" Thérèse later recalled. "Without saying a word I put my lips to her icy forehead. I do not remember having cried much, and I did not talk to anyone of all that filled my heart; I looked and listened in silence, and I saw many things they would have hidden from me.

"Once I found myself close to the coffin in the passage. I stood looking at it for a long time; I had never seen one before, but I knew what it was. I was so small that I had to lift up my head to see its whole length, and it seemed to me very big and very sad."

Later, when looking back on those traumatic times, Thérèse understood them to be the big turning point in her life. Everything was transformed. The carefree, happy days were over. The time of innocence was gone. Even her home and surroundings would soon change, when her father – within little more than two months – decided to leave Alençon and move to Lisieux to be close to Zélie's brother and his two young girls.

"I must tell you that after my mother's death my naturally happy disposition completely changed," Thérèse recollected. "Instead of being lively and demonstrative as I had been, I became timid, shy, and extremely sensitive; a look was enough to make me burst into tears. I could not bear to be noticed or to meet strangers, and was only at ease in my own family circle....That day, as I have said, began the second period of my life. It was the most sorrowful of all."

Following her mother's death, Thérèse found comfort in the companionship of her pets. She kept many in her family's new home in Lisieux.

A lively, loyal and affectionate dog named Tom entered the Little Flower's life when she was 11 years old. He wasn't, by any means, her first pet. She and her sister Céline already owned bluebirds and bantams, chickens and rabbits, including an unusual collection of silkworms. But nothing compared to the wonderful spaniel, with his long silky coat and drooping ears, who was selfless, loving and forgiving.

In 1884, Thérèse asked her father for "an animal with hair." He was baffled by the request, knowing that she already owned a collection of furry creatures. "But, my little queen," he said, "you have animals with hair; you have rabbits." She replied: "That's true, but I'd like an animal with hair that follows me everywhere and jumps around me." Hence, on 26 June 1884, the wonderful Tom entered the Martin household and became the best of friends with Thérèse.

There was no better place for Tom to move into than the Martin's new home, Les Buissonnets, in Lisieux. Not only was it substantial in size – with four rooms on the ground floor, four bedrooms and two dressing rooms – but it also had a small flowerbed at the front, a spacious garden at the rear, a vegetable garden, and many trees. There was a road outside, plenty of walks nearby and, most important of all, the attention of two doting sisters, Thérèse and Céline, who showered him with affection.

Tom and Thérèse soon became close companions. "Thérèse took a walk in the garden yesterday with Tom for more than half an hour because he had not gone out in the morning," the Little Flower's sister, Marie, once remarked in a letter. "She seemed happy to see herself followed so faithfully by her 'hairy beast.'"

The spaniel pined for his best friends, Thérèse and Céline, when they were away. On one occasion, while they were absent, their cousin visited the house and reported: "Tom does nothing but whimper day and night; he arouses deep pity in us." Another time, during that same vacation, their aunt wrote: "We always feel very sorry for Tom. He is crying all the time over your departure; however, Maria takes him out every day, she tells me. But see how faithful this beast is and how he loves you."

In later life, Thérèse would draw from the attributes and characteristics of her pets, including Tom, when outlining her little way. Being little was central to her thinking. She once described how the mother prioress and novice mistress in the Carmel were like "sportsmen" in pursuit of game. "But sportsmen are too big to be creeping through the cover," she pointed out. By comparison, "a little dog can push its way in anywhere." Just like Tom, she was "like a setter on the scent of game."

On another occasion, she wrote of her difficulties singing the *Canticle of Love*. Then she remembered what happened when a little linnet was brought into their house to live. It occupied the same room as a canary which had a beautiful voice. "This poor little prisoner, deprived of the teaching it should have received from its parents, and hearing the joyous trills of the canary from morning to night, tried hard to imitate them. A difficult task indeed for a linnet!

"It was delightful to follow the efforts of the poor little thing; his sweet voice found great difficulty in accommodating itself to the vibrant notes of his master, but he succeeded in time, and, to my great surprise, his song became exactly like the song of the canary," she remarked.

There were amusing moments, too, although some arose around tragedies involving the family pets. Once, a tiny female bluebird died, leaving behind her male companion. "Papa told us this morning that the remaining one appears very joyful at being rid of his wife, he is making never-ending chirps," Marie, one of the sisters, remarked in a letter.

Refusing to believe this interpretation, she added: "I believe the poor little husband was crying; birds are not like people, they cannot show their sorrow in another way." She continued: "Thérèse almost said a funeral prayer for the defunct" and concluded that "to soften bitter regrets they have decided to have it stuffed."

There was a further occasion, when Thérèse wrote about how Céline had killed most of her collection of silkworms. Having outlined, in a letter to her cousin, how the cousin must be "very happy not to be listening any longer to my sermons on death," Thérèse went on to do precisely that – deliver another sermon on death.

"I have to announce to you the death of *eight* of my silkworms," she wrote. "I have only *four* left. Céline lavished so much care on them that she made almost all of them die from sadness or a fatal seizure of apoplexy. I very much fear that the four that are left have caught the germ of their brothers' sickness and that they will follow them in death."

Perhaps the saddest story of all arose after Thérèse entered the Carmel and became a nun. Not only was she obliged to leave her beloved spaniel, Tom, behind, but her father soon became unwell and the family home had to be relinquished. "I was unable to refrain from crying when I saw them moving out these old remains from Les Buissonnets that recalled a thousand memories, and poor Tom following the wagons," one of the sisters wrote regarding the day the furniture was removed.

There was even worse to follow. Some of the furniture was given to cousins; more was donated to the Carmel. When the entourage arrived at the Carmel, Tom sensed the presence of his old friend. "Once inside the cloister, the faithful Tom raised his ears, then, looking in all directions as if to get his bearings, he sprang on his little mistress, leaping up at her face and making a thousand bounds in all directions," Céline observed.

Thérèse had to "lift her large veil and hide Tom under it, for he could not control his joy," the sister said. Obviously overcome, but unable to keep the dog in the convent, there was nothing Thérèse could do. "She was forced to tear herself away from all this, so great was her emotion," Céline pointed out. This was just one of many hardships Thérèse had to endure in the Carmel, but we are jumping ahead with the story. That event happened in October 1889. Before then, the Little Flower still had a lot of growing up to do in Lisieux.

One of the most important events linking Thérèse's move from childhood to maturity occurred in 1886, at Christmas – a time of year she always regarded as special.

Thérèse loved what she called "the beautiful feast of Christmas." As a child, she was showered with presents, pampered by her sisters and fussed over by her father. Les Buissonnets, where the family lived after Zélie's death, was perfect for celebrating the festive season. It was a warm, cosy home, with blazing fires, a busy kitchen and, most of all, a large fireplace where Thérèse and her sister Céline would place their shoes in the hope of receiving presents.

Unlike in Ireland, in Normandy it was shoes and not stockings that were placed by the chimney for the attention of St. Nicholas. After midnight Mass, the family would walk up the hill to their home, while Thérèse bristled with excitement at the thought of what lay in store. She was never disappointed. As she later explained, her father would "watch my enjoyment and hear my cries of delight at each fresh surprise that came from the magic shoes, and his pleasure added to mine."

Christmas 1886 turned out to be different. Even though she was 13 years old – and would be 14 in January – she was still being indulged like a child. Something happened that not only spoiled that Christmas but marked it out as a transforming moment in her life. The event occurred shortly after the family reached home following midnight Mass. Before looking at her presents, Thérèse went upstairs and, while on her way, overheard a remark made by her father.

"Really all this is too babyish for a big girl like Thérèse, and I hope it is the last year it will happen," her father said. Given that he seemed vexed and wasn't indulging his "little queen" as he normally would, his words "cut me to the quick," she remarked. Céline, who was with her, and who understood her sensitive nature, advised her to wait before going back downstairs as she would only cry. However, a defining moment had arrived and as the Little Flower later explained in *Story of a Soul*: "Thérèse was no longer the same – Jesus had changed her heart."

Choking back tears, Thérèse ran back down to the dining room, picked up her shoes, pulled out the presents, looking as happy as a queen. Her father laughed and seemed full of pleasure. Having witnessed what happened, Céline "thought she must be dreaming," the Little Flower later reflected. But a new reality had dawned. Thérèse was no longer a child; instead, she had gained "strength of mind." On that night, she remarked, all of her childhood's "innocent pleasures" were gone, and from then on her focus was on God.

It wasn't that Thérèse would never again love Christmas Day. It always retained its importance. After all, she had been born just over a week later, when her two eldest sisters were home on holiday from their boarding school, the Visitation Convent at Le Mans. She would also refer many times to the festive season in her autobiography, *Story of a Soul*. Indeed, so precious was Christmas that she had set it as the target date for her entry to the Carmel in Lisieux to become a nun.

Even today, reminders of Thérèse's festive joy can be seen at the family home, Les Buissonnets, in Lisieux. Among them are a toy kitchen stove with saucepans, a tea set and a young girl's doll which she received as presents. There is also a six-sided wood block puzzle, allowing for the creation of six pictorial images. Poignantly, the image left in place is of a Christmas scene with young children standing before a fireplace anticipating the presents they would receive. The box is inscribed in the hand of Céline, who notes that the puzzle belonged to Thérèse.

For Thérèse, however, her greatest memory of Christmas would be of the transforming event that occurred in 1886. From then on, she said, her mind developed, her sensitivity diminished and her desire for the salvation of souls increased day by day. Her childhood was behind her, and a new period in her life had begun.

"I was seized with a passionate desire for learning," she remarked, and "learnt more in a few months than I had in my whole school life." Nevertheless, there was still more schooling to be done despite what she referred to as her "long-desired miracle on Christmas Day, 1886."

Thérèse hated school, where she was badly bullied and became depressed. Her experiences there influenced her life, as we can see from her autobiography and a series of articles published in an old magazine with Irish connections.

As a young girl at school, Thérèse was sensitive and bright. These qualities helped her achieve high marks and academic success, but the accolades came at a price. She was badly bullied, cried often and couldn't wait to go home. "A little shade of sadness" would sometimes be seen on her features, one of her teachers noted. It was no surprise that she later referred to her school years as "the saddest of my life."

Thérèse entered the Abbey of Notre Dame du Pré in October 1881. Run by the Benedictine nuns, it was a prestigious school, offering facilities to boarders and day pupils since the late seventeenth century. Set in an austere-looking building in Lisieux, it educated some of the finest French young ladies of its time. Their pedigree, unfortunately, didn't always stop them from bullying their classmates.

After initially being taught at home, Thérèse was enrolled at the school as a day pupil at the age of eight and a half. "The girls of my class were all older than myself; one of them was fourteen, and, though not clever, she knew how to impose on the little ones," she recalled in *Story of a Soul*. "Seeing me so young, nearly always first in class, and a favourite with all the nuns, she was jealous, and used to pay me out in a thousand ways.

"Naturally timid and sensitive, I did not know how to defend myself, and could only cry in silence. Céline and my elder sisters did not know of my grief, and, not being advanced enough in virtue to rise above these troubles, I suffered considerably. Every evening I went home, and then my spirits rose. I would climb onto Papa's knee, telling him what marks I had, and his caresses made me forget all my troubles."

By remarkable good fortune, Thérèse's problems at school were chronicled by one of the Benedictine nuns – a former teacher – in a series of little-known articles published in 1934. The articles were featured in a magazine called *The Far East*, which promoted the work of Columban missionary priests and sisters, who were mostly Irish. Founded in Ireland, in 1916, their society was originally known as the Maynooth Mission to China, hence the name of its magazine.

"What a beautiful, winsome child our Thérèse was!" the nun wrote in the March 1934 issue of *The Far East* regarding the new entrant to the school. "A real little angel, with her long, fair, golden curls, framing such a sweet face; her pure brow, her clear eyes, her indescribable smile....With all that, a calmness – one might almost say, gravity – of manner was joined in her to a childlike grace, in perfect harmony."

Thérèse was excellent at her studies. Her best subjects were history and geography; she also stood out in religion class where her teacher referred to her as his "little Doctor of Theology". Thérèse recalled in *Story of a Soul* how she won a silver coin for her first essay, receiving maximum marks. Not only did she put the coin in her money box for the poor, but "nearly every Thursday I was able to increase the fund," she explained. She had "good marks constantly, everywhere and in everything," her teacher noted.

Her teacher was also aware of the bullying. Referring to a pupil who was older, "very backward" and of "limited intelligence," she explained that "it is not surprising that she became jealous of the successes of her youngest companion and of the affectionate regard in which this companion was held among the nuns." Unfortunately, as so often happens, the nun said that "these are some of the difficulties that occur in every educational institution" and explained how "Providence was preparing the young schoolgirl for the truly great and painful trials that she was to meet later on." It wasn't exactly an enlightened response.

The impact of the bullying on Thérèse was significant. She never participated in games and, instead, would find little dead birds who she would bury under the lime trees or at the foot of the pear tree in the school. "Our cemetery was there in the corner formed by the chapel, close to the entrance to the cellar," she explained. She also came to suffer from what was called "scruples", which, in effect, is referred to as obsessive compulsive disorder today. It involves sufferers being plunged into paralysing anxiety and distress over issues like sin and guilt.

The onset of her illness didn't stop Thérèse from occasionally playing the rogue during her time at school. Once, on her way home, she and her cousin shut their eyes and pretended to be blind. "For a short while, all went well," she recalled, "and we enjoyed walking with our eyes shut; but presently we both fell over some boxes standing at a shop door and knocked them down. The shopkeeper came out in a rage to replace them, but the would-be blind pair picked themselves up and ran off as fast as they could, with eyes wide open."

Given her intelligence and mastery of subjects, she also occasionally whispered answers to other pupils who hadn't done their homework or grasped some facts. This was regarded as a breach of discipline at the school. Eventually, she developed severe troubles with her conscience over the issue, further increasing her anxiety. "My scrupulosity finished by making me ill," she observed, "and I had to be taken from school at the age of thirteen."

Thérèse was withdrawn from the Benedictine Abbey by her father at Easter 1886. As her former teacher put it, her father decided that "his little daughter was no longer physically able for the regular classwork" and "resolved that she should finish her education by means of private tuition in town." Ironically, given her early departure – with two full years still to go, along with the last few months of her current year – the way was paved for her entry to the Carmel at the age of 15.

Thérèse returned to the school for one last visit, moving from one classroom to another, and speaking to the teachers. Most were unaware that the visit was to be her last. She also met the teacher who wrote the articles in 1934, but she never told her it was her final goodbye. "She seemed a little embarrassed and so was I," the teacher explained. "On leaving, she embraced me affectionately. As for what we said, alas, I cannot recall it now." And then she was gone, out onto the Rue Gustave David and, not long after, to the Carmel in Lisieux. The teacher never saw her again.

Thérèse's family were long aware of her yearning to take the veil. Her wish was not easily achieved.

Thérèse Martin seemed destined to become a nun. Her aunt, Marie-Louise, had taken her vows as a Visitation sister. Her mother, Zélie, had wanted to do so, too, but was turned away on health grounds. Her father, Louis, would have become a monk but was rejected for not having Latin. Topping things off, Thérèse's four sisters all became nuns. With Zélie and Louis at the helm, the family were like a mini religious order.

"The good God gave me a father and a mother more worthy of heaven than of earth," Thérèse later wrote of her parents. She certainly had a point. Religion dominated household proceedings. There were morning Masses, daily prayers, Sunday devotions, and visits to Aunt Marie-Louise at the Visitation convent. The family lived good and righteous lives, observing Church rules and practising charity towards those less fortunate than themselves.

The Martins were genuinely holy – pious and dedicated to God. Zélie, on giving birth, prayed that each child would be consecrated to God. To become a priest or nun would be the highest honour. "My parents always seemed to me to be saints," one of the girls, Pauline, later said. "We were filled with respect and admiration for them. Sometimes I asked myself if there could be others like them on earth. I never saw any such round me."

To understand the Martin girls, we must also understand the times. Young women's options in life were limited. For many, the choice outside of marriage was convent life, minding aged parents or emigration. Middle-class girls – often educated and from farm backgrounds – took the respectable option and entered cloistered life. It was not unusual for whole families of girls, generation after generation, to take the veil.

In Ireland, during Thérèse's life, there were eight times more nuns than there had been 60 years earlier. Many of these 8,000 nuns were forced out of farms by changing agricultural practices, including the mechanisation of milking and butter-making and the commercialisation of egg production. Having a priest in the family might have once been the ultimate symbol of prestige; having a daughter who was a "Bride of Christ" had become prestigious, too.

Pauline was the first Martin girl to join a convent. Thérèse learned of her imminent departure in the worst possible way, overhearing a conversation between Pauline and another sister, Marie. She was devastated, and immediately ran to her bedroom and cried. "It was as if a sword were buried in my heart," she remarked.

Not only did Thérèse lose a dear sister, but she also lost her third mother. It was Pauline who had replaced Thérèse's wet nurse Rose Taillé and her deceased mother Zélie. She had schooled her young sister at home, guiding her, comforting her, and providing motherly love. "I have asked myself many times how you were able to bring me up with so much love and tenderness and without spoiling me," Thérèse remarked years later.

Pauline entered the Carmel as a postulant on 2 October 1882. Towards the end of that day, Thérèse spoke to her sister through the grille. "I was weak, so weak that I considered it a great grace to have been able to support a trial that seemed to be far above my strength," Thérèse reflected. She became more determined than ever to become a nun. "It was by your example," she said of Pauline, "which drew me to the Spouse of Virgins."

Four years later – in August 1886 – the next Martin daughter, Marie, announced that she too had decided to join the Carmel. Thérèse was about to lose her "fourth mother". Since Pauline's departure, Marie had taken on the maternal role. "It was Marie who guided, consoled, and aided me in the practise of virtue," Thérèse commented. "She was indispensable to me....I loved her so much I couldn't live without her."

The event changed her life. "As soon as I learned of Marie's decision, I made up my mind not to look for enjoyment in this world any longer," a devastated Thérèse said. Eventually, her other two sisters – Céline and Léonie – also became nuns, the former in the Carmel and the latter at the Monastery of the Visitation at Caen. By then, however, Thérèse too had become a nun, albeit with difficulty.

Two seemingly insurmountable problems were blocking Thérèse's entry to the Carmel in Lisieux. To begin with, she wished to enter as a 15-year-old, even though the rule was that no one could enter before the age of 21. Second, it was stipulated that no convent should contain more than two people from the same family. It was the former rule that was causing problems, with Pauline relaying news that the superior would not permit Thérèse to enter until her twenty-first birthday.

Thérèse and her father decided to appeal to the bishop in Bayeux. On 31 October 1887, they travelled to the bishop's house to plead her case. The meeting had an uncomfortable beginning. The bishop offered Thérèse an armchair, but she refused the offer politely; the chair seemed too big and too grand. He insisted she take it. "I did so without any more hesitation," she wrote in *Story of a Soul*, "and was mortified to see him take an ordinary chair while I was buried in an enormous seat that would comfortably have held four children like me."

Thérèse made her case, arguing that she had wanted to give herself to God since the time she was three. After a lengthy discussion, the bishop, who treated her kindly, said he was travelling to Lisieux the next week and added "I will talk to the superior about you." After ushering his two visitors into the garden, the bishop was then informed by Thérèse's father of a trick his daughter had used to impress him.

"Papa told him that, to make myself look older, I had put up my hair for the first time that very morning," Thérèse recalled in her book. "This was not forgotten, for I know that even now, whenever the bishop tells anyone about his 'little daughter,' he always repeats the story about her hair. I must say I should prefer my little secret to have been kept."

Thérèse and Louis Martin returned to Lisieux without a favourable answer. "It seemed to me as though my future were shattered forever," Thérèse remarked. Or was it? The bishop may not have been entirely helpful, she concluded, but there was always someone else to appeal to – the pope!

In late 1887, *The Cork Examiner* reported on what would be one of the most significant events in Thérèse Martin's life. It occurred when she was aged 14.

The Saturday edition of *The Cork Examiner*, on 31 December 1887, carried what seemed to be a relatively insignificant story about a small disturbance in Rome. The report referred to a pilgrimage from northern France – incorporating people from Bayeux and Lisieux – that had arrived some weeks earlier. It had come to the Eternal City to celebrate the fiftieth anniversary of Pope Leo XIII's ordination to the priesthood.

On emerging from their train, the French pilgrims had been met by "a motley crowd of radicals," shouting "Down with Leo XIII" and "Death to the clericals," among other loud chants. Police had arrived and 12 protestors had been arrested. The newspaper report added: "The pilgrimage was received in papal audience on Sunday, November 20th, and left Rome the following Thursday, after a short visit, *ad interim*, to Naples."

Unknown to *The Cork Examiner*, the young Thérèse Martin was on board that train, along with her father and sister Céline. She had arrived in Rome determined to ask the pope if he would permit her to become a nun. It was a foolhardy plan, even if the group she was with was being afforded a papal audience. To begin with, it was forbidden to speak to the pope or ask him questions. She was also only 14 years of age and a request to join the nuns had previously been turned down.

Emerging from the train, Thérèse joined the throng of pilgrims arriving to celebrate Pope Leo XIII's golden jubilee. People from many nationalities were already in the city, including the Irish. Back home, other people from Ireland were packing their bags and preparing to leave for Rome. One Irish group had booked their places on a "Spiritual Pilgrimage" – with the promise of gaining indulgences – which was promoted in Irish newspapers and organised via London. Numerous bishops and archbishops – from Dublin, Cork and Galway, among other dioceses – were also either there or on their way.

After exploring the many sights of Rome – the Coliseum, Catacombs, Church of St. Agnes and the former site of the tomb of St. Cecilia – the French pilgrims arrived at the Vatican for their audience with the pope. The date was 20 November 1887, the same date – and the same event – that *The Cork Examiner* had covered in their article. "On it depended my vocation," Thérèse would later say of that fateful day.

After Mass in the pope's private chapel, the papal audience began. It must have been a daunting occasion. The pope, wearing a white cassock and cape, sat in his raised chair. He was surrounded by Church dignitaries. A lean man, with white hair, he had once been known for his impetuosity but had calmed down.

"He has a classic mouth," an eminent French author wrote, using the flowery prose of the time. "His smile does not possess that sardonic Voltairian expression found in so many of his photographs. On the contrary, it is rather gentle and paternal. His eyes are very black and brilliant. His features, ascetic and strongly marked, have become benevolent and engaging. Like St. Francis de Sales, who was born dogmatic and choleric, but who became, by continual self-subjection, an angel of sweetness, Leo XIII, on being made pope, must have overcome, or at least subdued, an impetuous character."

Thérèse stood there and watched as Christ's Vicar was approached by one pilgrim after another. Each one knelt and kissed his foot and hand. He then blessed them, after which two of his Noble Guards signalled for the visitor to move on. There was deathly silence; no one spoke.

The Little Flower's turn was coming soon. As if sensing what was about to happen, the Vicar-General of Bayeux, who was standing on the pope's right-hand side, spoke loudly and said no one was to address the Holy Father. Thérèse's heart beat faster. She didn't know what to do. Turning to Céline, her sister, she asked for advice. "Speak," Céline instantly replied.

Thérèse was suddenly on her knees before Pope Leo XIII. She kissed his foot. He held out his hand to be kissed. At that moment, she raised her eyes, which were filled with tears, and spoke. "Holy Father," she said, "I have a great favour to ask you." He leaned forward, his face beside hers, his piercing black eyes staring into her soul. "Holy Father," she repeated, "in honour of your jubilee, will you allow me to enter the Carmel when I am fifteen?"

The Vicar-General of Bayeux interrupted. Annoyed, he said abruptly that Thérèse had hoped to join the Carmelites and the superiors of the Carmel were examining her request. "Well, my child," the pontiff said, "do whatever the superiors decide." Placing her hands on the pope's knee, Thérèse tried one more time. "Holy Father, if only you say 'yes,' everyone else would agree."

The pope stared at her and responded: "Well, well! You will enter if it is God's will." Seeing that she was about to speak again – and with her hands still clasped on the pope's knee – the Noble Guards and the Vicar-General stepped forward to move her away. As they were about to force her to rise, Pope Leo XIII placed his hand on her lips, lifted his hand to bless her, and gazed after her intently as she left the room in tears.

Thus it was, in 1887, that Christ's representative on earth met a future saint and a yet-to-be-crowned Little Flower of Lisieux. Despite the tears, Thérèse was relieved. She felt an "inward peace," as she put it. She had tried her best. "This peace," however, only "dwelt in the depths of my soul – on the surface all was bitterness; and Jesus was silent – absent it would seem, for nothing revealed that He was there," she later reflected.

Thérèse's visit to the Vatican would long be recalled, not just in *The Cork Examiner* but by the religious in Rome, one of whom, on hearing of her conversation with the pope, said: "This kind of thing is not seen in Italy." Her discussion also became a talking point with her fellow pilgrims, with at least one of them referring to her, from then on, as "our little Carmelite."

Later, when the dust settled, it seemed that on that November day, in 1887, someone must have been watching over Thérèse after all. Perhaps, as she had hoped, it was God, or maybe the pope intervened, who knows. Either way, on Monday, 9 April 1888, on the Feast of the Annunciation, Thérèse entered the Lisieux Carmel at the extraordinarily young age of 15 years and three months.

Living conditions were harsh for Thérèse at the Carmel. Irish-American author Dorothy Day addressed them in her book on the saint.

Meagre rations of food, a bed made of three planks, no heat in the convent except for a small stove in one room, and constant prayer and penance, were all experienced by Thérèse on entering the Carmel in Lisieux. She wore a habit of coarse serge, rope sandals on her feet, and stockings of rough muslin. Rising at 5.45 am in winter and 4.45 am in summer, most of her day was devoted to work or prayer. There was no let up apart from two brief periods of recreation.

The work was tough and tedious – washing floors, sweeping rooms, cleaning laundry, caring for the dining room, kitchen

40

and sacristy. Rinsing clothes in cold water chilled you to the bone in winter. Chapped red hands, swollen and blistered with chilblains, were common. The laundry was steaming hot in the summer. It wasn't just for one day, or one week, or one month that these chores stretched before you. It was forever, until death released you to the arms of God.

Matters weren't helped by the age structure and small number of nuns in the Carmel. The complement of around 20 sisters – all crammed in together – reflected varying age groups, young and old. Some were fresh-faced and healthy. Others were infirm and mentally confused. Those who were ill needed looking after. Not everyone was capable of work. The result was that most of the workload fell on the novices and nuns of a younger age.

"Thérèse always tried to take the most difficult tasks, feeling that it was the part of charity to do so since she would be saving another sister the hard labour," the Brooklyn-born Irish-American author Dorothy Day, who was born the year Thérèse died, wrote in her book on the saint. "It was the same with the hot, steamy laundry in summer. When there was a choice of work, she took the hardest, not only as a penance but as an act of loving kindness, a practice in love."

The cold was Thérèse's worst enemy. It chilled her to the bone. It was sometimes so cold that she feared she could die. The chapel, where hour after hour was spent in prayer, was icy. Her cell was unheated. Things weren't helped by the Normandy weather, which could dip below freezing in winter, bringing snow and ice. The solitary reprieve was from the fire in the recreation room, but access was restricted to a few hours a day. It was only in the recreation room that the nuns could speak; otherwise, the rule called for complete silence.

The prayers were equally tough. Six or seven hours of prayers were said daily. The Office included four hours of Prime, Terce, Sext and None celebrated in the morning. Vespers was said in the afternoon, Compline at day's end, Matins at the beginning of the night, followed by Lauds. "Unlike the secular, or diocesan, clergy, the monk and the nun are obliged to chant the Office," Day noted. "This in itself is a physical work, taking the strength and the breath of the body."

Matters weren't helped by a prioress who treated Thérèse harshly. Her name was Mother Marie de Gonzague. She would later tell Monsignor Laveille, Vicar-General of Meaux, that she had sought to "try" Thérèse by treating her with a certain level of severity and indifference. This harsh treatment, she told him, had been painful but never stopped Thérèse from being obedient.

The prioress was adept at handing out criticism. One day, Thérèse overlooked a cobweb when cleaning a hall. The prioress was incensed. In front of other sisters, she said: "The cloisters are obviously swept by a 15-year-old; it is a disgrace! Go and sweep that cobweb away and in the future be more careful!" She also scolded Thérèse during sessions concerning spiritual direction. "The worst of it was I did not know how to correct my faults," Thérèse would later remark.

There was no talking back, no arguing, disagreeing or contradicting. The rule was to accept criticism, even if falsely based, kiss the ground in humility, and offer up the sacrifice to God. In *Story of a Soul*, Thérèse relates how, one day, such an event occurred.

"A small jar, left behind a window, was found broken," she recalled. "No one knew who had put it there, but our mistress was displeased, and, thinking I was to blame in leaving it about, told me I was very untidy and must be more careful in future. Without answering, I kissed the ground and promised to be more observant....I had to console myself with the thought that at the Day of Judgement all would be known."

This gruelling, relentless life continued apace even as Thérèse's subsequent illness progressed. "She went on washing windows, washing clothes and the work was laborious indeed," Dorothy Day noted in her book, *Thérèse*. "Sometimes she could scarcely walk up the stairs she was so exhausted, but went from step to step, breathing heavily, scarcely able to lift one foot after the other....She never complained, she went on with the work of the day in chapel and out of it, and said nothing."

Yet here in this cold, austere convent, cut off from the public and confined with a small group of nuns, Thérèse found the spiritual salvation she so desperately sought. "Thérèse had the wit to see that these pinpricks, indeed they might be called dagger thrusts, were of the stuff suffering is made of," Dorothy Day concluded. "Thérèse accepted it all as something of which she was in need. She knew she had 'to die in order to live'.... her vocation was indeed tried."

Thérèse developed her little way in the Carmel. This simple, direct spiritual code became one of the most important religious philosophies of modern times.

Thérèse always wanted to become a saint. There was one big problem – she didn't feel she had the sanctity required. She had accomplished no great deeds, climbed no spiritual mountains, and didn't have the piety or purity of one so glorified and holy. "There exists between them and me," she once wrote, "the same difference as we see in nature between a mountain with its summit hidden in the clouds and the grain of sand trodden under the feet of passers-by."

Rather than being discouraged, she devised another route to sainthood. She called it her little way. It was, she said, a way for little people like herself. "I cannot make myself greater," she reasoned; instead, her goal was to "bear with myself just as I am with all my imperfections." Do the little things you do every day, but do them with love and in the best way you can, and offer them up to God. "What matters in life is not great deeds, but great love," she argued.

Her autobiography, *Story of a Soul*, chronicled how Thérèse practised her little way in the Carmel. On the surface, the philosophy was far from profound. She cared for the altar, ran the sacristy, served food in the refectory, cleaned clothes in the laundry, looked after her fellow sisters, adhered to the rules, prayed, meditated and practised humility – all the everyday things she was asked to do.

But that was precisely her point. "In my 'little way' everything is most ordinary," she explained. It's just that those tasks are done with humility and commitment, and done to please God. By those standards, everyone can adhere to the little way. "All that I do, little souls must be able to do likewise," she pointed out. It was "a new way, very short, very straight, a little path," designed for little people like herself.

There was always something charmingly simple and innocent in the analogies Thérèse used to explain her reasoning. Things were no different when it came to her little way. "One day a horse was standing in front of the garden gate, and preventing us from getting through," she remarked of an event from her childhood. "My companions talked to him and tried to make him move off, but while they were still talking I quietly slipped between his legs....Such is the advantage of remaining small!"

What else can a small child do? It shows love for its parents in simple, trusting, innocent ways. Its actions aren't complex or awe-inspiring. Instead, it declares its love in the most uncomplicated fashion – by smiling, caressing, using words of affection, and directing its actions to those who matter most in its life. "I have always therefore remained little, occupying myself solely in gathering flowers of love and sacrifice and offering them to the good God for his pleasure," she remarked.

In her time in the Carmel, Thérèse was determined to retain her smallness. Not only did she practise daily life – her little chores and relationships with others – to perfection, but she offered everything up to God. She responded to suffering with a smile; every little act she did was performed with love. She also practised humility and self-deprecation up to the time of her death.

One story, in particular, summed up her sense of "littleness". The story involved a sister who was temporarily caring for Thérèse in her final days. On being offered some food, which Thérèse was aware would cause her to vomit, she graciously declined it.

The sister was annoyed and afterwards said to a companion: "I do not know why they talk so much of Soeur Thérèse de l'Enfant Jésus; she does nothing remarkable; one cannot even say that she is exactly a good religious." When the Little Flower later heard of the remark, her face lit up and she smiled. "To hear on my bed of death that I am not a good religious, what joy!" she said. She was "little" right to the last.

Looking back, in some ways Thérèse's philosophy was far from new. She described how she drew its inspiration from the Bible. "Whoever is a little one, let him come to me," she had read in the sacred text. And how does God deal with little ones? Once again, Thérèse was pleased with the answer: "As a mother comforts her son, so I will comfort you."

She also undoubtedly drew inspiration from the simplicity of the early monks and saints – many of them Irish – who had practiced their own little way. Living lives of self-sacrifice and love, they had directed their actions and energies to the love of others and, above all, to the love of God. In that sense, she was not unlike St. Brigid – "Mary of the Gael" – who sought little for herself and dedicated her life to God by caring for his creation and acting with grace and simplicity.

In time, Thérèse's little way became a code of practise for the good and the great. A succession of popes, authors, statesmen and philosophers, along with millions of ordinary people, were influenced by what she had to say. It was an extraordinary achievement for a young woman who had lived a simple, cloistered life, away from the noise of the world, yet who made such an extraordinary mark in the few years preceding her death at the age of 24.

On 30 September 1897, Thérèse died at the Carmel in Lisieux. She died from a disease rampant in Ireland. The disease was commonly referred to as "consumption" but is now known as tuberculosis.

At the stroke of midnight, on Holy Thursday 1896, Thérèse arrived at her cell in the Carmel. She put out her lamp, lay down on her bed and placed her head on the pillow. Instantly, she felt a warm stream of liquid entering her mouth. She knew something was wrong, but decided to wait until morning to find out what had happened.

When she awoke, at five o'clock, she recalled the event of the night before. Rising from her bed, she walked to the window and discovered that her handkerchief was drenched in blood. Most people would feel terror, but Thérèse was overjoyed. This, after all, was Good Friday – the day when Jesus died – and she knew that she had taken a first step towards joining him in heaven.

Back in 1896, everyone knew the significance of coughing up blood. It was often a sign of pulmonary consumption: that dark, insidious disease that ate away the lungs and, for many, brought a painful end. Like Ireland – where the plague was rampant – France saw hundreds of thousands of its citizens "consumed" by premature and gradual decay, followed by death. "In the vast multitude of cases," as one Irish newspaper put it, "complete cure is hopeless" and the odds against survival are one-sided.

After rising on that Good Friday morning, Thérèse downplayed what had happened the previous night. Although she was permitted to undertake the penances and workload required for that day, she was clearly in trouble. That afternoon, a novice noticed her cleaning windows, with her face flushed and body exhausted. She refused help, arguing that her fatigue was nothing compared to the suffering Jesus had experienced on that fateful day.

Her health deteriorated over time. Each night, she climbed the stairs to her wooden bed, drained and out of breath. She would pause on each step. It took her an hour to undress. On entering her bed, she would lie there in pain, her sleep disturbed, her strength slipping away. She refused to be accompanied and cared for, saying she was happy to suffer alone.

In time, she did need assistance, particularly when walking in the garden. One day, while doing so – and accompanied by one of the sisters – she noticed a hen protecting its chicks under a wing. The sight made her cry. Tears flowed down her face. She asked her companion to help her back inside. On reaching her cell, she explained that the hen had reminded her of God, who had protected her under his wing. She was overcome by His sweetness.

In July 1897, Thérèse was removed to the infirmary, where her health deteriorated further. By mid-August, she could no longer receive Holy Communion and was unable to do so up to the time of her death. Her pain was intense, although her face wore an expression of bliss. The greater the pain, the greater the joy she felt. She offered the suffering up to God. The doctor expressed his admiration, saying: "I have never seen anyone suffer so intensely with such a look of supernatural joy."

There were consolations that kept her spirits alive. Friends delivered bouquets of flowers from the world outside. A little robin kept her company and would flutter around her bed. On one occasion, the nun who ran the infirmary, recognising that she was burning with fever and parched with thirst, brought her a drink. She was deeply moved and thanked Jesus for his tenderness and loving care.

All the time, her suffering intensified. She found it difficult to speak. Even to hear someone else whispering caused pain. She was weak and tired, yet she never ceased smiling. Her only worry was that she was a burden to the nuns. One of the sisters once asked her what she said when she prayed to Jesus. "I say nothing – I only love Him!" she replied.

The end came on Thursday, 30 September 1897. Outside the Carmel, the long warm days of summer were being replaced by softer weather and autumnal skies. The woods and hedgerows were ablaze with glowing colours. Farmers were preparing for winter, while offering cider for sale at their farm gates. This was a season so loved by Thérèse, but not this year.

For many weeks, she had been immobile in her bed. She was, she said, experiencing "pure agony, without a ray of consolation." Knowing she was going to die, she asked her sister Pauline – the mother prioress – to help her prepare for death. Pauline reassured her she was ready to appear before God.

Late that afternoon, her fellow sisters gathered around her and she thanked them for all they had done. She did so with a sweet smile. Clearly in pain, sweating and trembling, she clasped a crucifix in her hands, awaiting her final moments.

At 6 pm, the Angelus bells rang out in the convent. Thérèse stared at the statue of the Immaculate Virgin, the Star of the Sea. An hour later, at a few minutes past 7 pm, she turned to her sister and asked was she about to die. Pauline told her she was. Looking at her crucifix, she uttered her last words – "My God, I....love....Thee!" She then sank back in her bed, with her head inclined to the right.

With one last exertion, Thérèse raised herself up, opened her eyes and, as if being called by some distant voice, stared at a space above Our Lady's statue. A look of happiness and peace came over her face. Once more, she lay back on her pillow and, aged 24, passed on to another life.

A SOUL TAKES FLIGHT

It was highly significant that *The Irish Ecclesiastical Record* endorsed Thérèse of Lisieux in its August 1912 edition. This was, after all, a conservative Catholic Church-sanctioned publication, targeted at a clerical audience. That it offered enthusiastic support to the Little Flower – who was a woman, young, relatively uneducated and with a simple writing style – was remarkable in the extreme.

Although published soon after Thérèse's death, the author of the article noted her numerous miracles. He also remarked how her little way was appealing to many – "to the child at school and to the teacher, to the servant maid and the worker," among others. Readers of her autobiography, he said, had "drawn profit from her pages."

Nowhere was this more evident than in Ireland. Around the time the article was written, many Irish people were reading the Little Flower's book. More were on their way to Lisieux as pilgrims. All were being captivated by her miracles and cures.

In 1911, Irish newspapers reported a miracle attributed to the Little Flower. The coverage was responsible for the growth in Ireland of devotion to the future saint.

The first reports detailing a miraculous cure associated with Thérèse of Lisieux surfaced in Irish newspapers in late 1911. The story concerned a woman who had suffered from a cancerous tumour which disappeared following prayers to the deceased nun. Not only did the tumour and associated symptoms vanish, but her doctor declared the recovery to be "nothing short of a miracle."

The woman in question was a Glaswegian named Helen Dorans. Widowed and with a large family, she lived in one of the city's southern suburbs, Kinning Park. Her symptoms first surfaced when she noticed a pain in the left side of her abdomen. She was soon unable to function properly and could only get a fitful night's sleep. A tumour was diagnosed. Within a few years, it was growing so fast – and had become so large – that a decision was taken to remove it.

The woman entered the city's Western Infirmary at the end of April 1909, where she came under the care of Professor Samson Gemmell, one of the finest physicians in Scotland. After an examination, he told her the bad news. The tumour was not only cancerous but inoperable, and any attempt to remove it would kill her, he said. Other members of the medical staff concurred. Around mid-May, she returned home.

Her regular doctor explained that no more could be done and placed her on pain-relief medication. He also outlined to her family that she would become progressively weaker, eventually slide into unconsciousness and die. The family was distraught. By August, his prediction was proving to be remarkably accurate – she hadn't eaten solid food for ten weeks and was on the verge of death.

By this stage, Mrs. Dorans was resigned to her fate. She was losing her sight and could no longer distinguish people about her or objects in her room. A woman of faith, and a practising Catholic, she hoped that death would come soon. Unknown to her, however, members of her family and a number of friends were praying for the exact opposite to happen. They were looking for a miracle.

They appealed initially to the Sacred Heart and Our Lady of Lourdes, but without any success. Mrs. Dorans' condition worsened, and for four days she sank rapidly. She was given the last rites. It was around this time that a nun from the Sisters of Mercy – an order founded in Dublin in 1831 – suggested a novena to the Little Flower. The events that followed were extraordinary.

On the night of Thursday, 26 August 1909, it was clear that Mrs. Dorans had only hours to live. Around 11 pm, she fell asleep. She later explained that, about 5.30 in the morning, she felt pressure on her shoulders as if someone was leaning over her. She also detected a sweet, warm breath on her face. It led her to believe that she was in the presence of something divine.

The woman slowly opened her eyes. To her astonishment, she could see all the objects in her room. The pain had disappeared. After drifting back to sleep again, for approximately 20 minutes, she awoke and placed her hand on her abdomen to feel the tumour. It was no longer there.

Her general practitioner – Dr. Carmichael – was summoned immediately. He was mystified by what he encountered. Mrs. Dorans' swelling had vanished and the tumour – which had once been the size of an orange – was now the size of a marble. Even that tiny growth would disappear within 24 hours. His patient's general demeanour had also dramatically improved.

That date – 27 August 1909 – was a turning point in the life of Helen Dorans. She recovered her strength and was able, once more, to look after her large family. She even provided care by day and night to her sick friends. Her recovery was complete, with an X-ray taken a year later confirming that the malignancy was gone.

Most importantly, her miracle was given medical credence by the eminent surgeon, Thomas Colvin, of the University of Glasgow, who examined Mrs. Dorans in late June 1910. His report made for interesting reading: "I found her in excellent health. All her organs were sound and free from disease, or any tendency to disease. I made a special examination of the abdomen, and found it normal. There was not the slightest trace of any tumour, or any growth, or any abnormality, to be made out either in the left lumbar region, or in the left iliac region, or in any region of the abdomen."

Dr. Colvin also assessed the claim that the disappearance of the tumour was miraculous or at the very least inexplicable. He concluded that a cancerous tumour had once existed; all the evidence pointed in that direction. He continued: "A cancerous tumour invariably kills the patient sooner or later, and why this cancerous tumour did not kill Mrs. Dorans, but on the contrary entirely disappeared, leaving no trace of its existence, is beyond the ken of medical science."

It was no surprise that the story, once reported, captured the imagination of the Irish public. Up to its publication in late August 1911, Irish people had little interest in the Little Flower. Indeed, most had never even heard of her. Following the first headline declaring "Remarkable Cure" all that would change. By 1912, she became a regular object of interest. And it was all down to that moment, in August 1909, when an event occurred in Glasgow that one doctor described as "nothing short of a miracle."

A new translation of *Story of a Soul* arrived in Ireland in 1912, stimulating enormous interest in the future saint.

The first popular English translation of *Story of a Soul* was published in 1912. Before then, the autobiography was available only in French or in relatively inaccessible English formats. The new version, which trickled into Irish bookshops towards the end of the year, produced an instant reaction. Sales boomed as newspaper coverage clicked into gear.

Irish people who were fluent in French could have read the book as far back as 1898. In that year, Mother Agnès – Thérèse's sister, Pauline – had brought out a limited edition of the manuscript primarily for other Carmelite convents or people of religious significance. Interest in the book was phenomenal. One edition led to the next, and soon the book was being translated into other languages. It wasn't until 1912 that British publishers Burns, Oates & Washbourne Ltd. produced the first widely distributed and genuinely popular version for public sale.

Initial reviews in Ireland were ecstatic. The *Irish Independent* praised it highly. "Worthy of being placed side by side with the most striking of the *Confessions of the Saints*," it declared. *The Cork Examiner* was equally effusive. "The biography of a singularly favoured Servant of God, written by her own hand, is a document the value of which no human standard can appraise," it remarked.

Another popular newspaper of the time, *The Freeman's Journal* – which was Ireland's first nationalist newspaper, later incorporated into the *Irish Independent* – praised the book's presentation: "The volume is beautifully printed and bound, with gilt title and gilt border." Even *The Southern Star* got in on the act, with its reviewer stating: "Her autobiography, from a purely literary point of view, cannot be ignored even by those outside the fold of the Catholic Church."

Bookshops quickly offered the title for sale. Retailing for six shillings, it became an immediate success. Among those selling the book was James Duffy & Co., Ltd., Westmoreland Street, Dublin, whose owner, from County Monaghan, had risen from a hedge-school education to become one of the most prominent publishers and book retailers in the country. At one stage, he employed 120 people in his many Dublin businesses.

Brisk sales were also reported in Cork, where Con O'Keeffe promoted the book from his premises at 70 George's Street, which is now Oliver Plunkett Street. At the time, he employed a young salesman, Liam Ruiséal, who would later go on to set up his own bookshop just down the street. It was in O'Keeffe's, in 1916, that author Frank O'Connor first discovered the writing talents of one of his idols, Daniel Corkery. How many discovered Thérèse's autobiography there, we do not know, although we can deduce that the number must have been high.

Interest in the book was helped, no doubt, by the provision of an indulgence of 200 days to those who read it. Such indulgences – promising remission of punishment in the afterlife for sins committed on earth – were commonplace. For example, Pope Pius XII offered three years indulgence for people who read the Bible for at least a quarter of an hour. Five hundred days was promised to the faithful who read verses of the Gospel, kissed the Gospel Book, and recited certain invocations. The 200 days for reading Thérèse, while no doubt welcomed by some, was paltry by comparison!

The book also did very well for its publishers, the esteemed publishing house Burns, Oates & Washbourne. The company – British and Roman Catholic – was a story in itself. It had been founded in 1835 by James Burns, a Scottish-born convert from Presbyterianism to Catholicism. He, in turn, had been joined by William Wilfred Oates, who was another convert to the Catholic faith. Just to add to the firm's Rome-oriented ethos, Burns' wife converted, as well. It was no surprise that the firm was designated "Publishers to the Holy See" by Pope Leo XIII.

There was no doubt regarding Burns, Oates & Washbourne's commitment to the title. It was a de luxe edition, well-bound and skilfully illustrated. As one reviewer put it: "In letterpress and illustrations the volume reflects the highest credit upon the well-known publishing firm." Another reviewer added: "To the Catholic publishers we must pay the highest tribute of praise for the manner in which they have produced this volume. They have reached in its production the high-water mark of refined taste and artistic excellence."

The impact of the book in Ireland was enormous. A flurry of activity followed its publication. Within weeks, numerous articles about the Little Flower appeared in the press. Religious magazines and journals featured her story. *The Irish Rosary* – "a first-class monthly of Catholic tone," as one critic called it – provided readers with insights to her life. So also did *The Irish Ecclesiastical Record.*

Public lectures were held throughout the country. One of them – in St. Joseph's Parochial Hall, Terenure, Dublin – was packed to the rafters for what *The Freeman's Journal* called a most fascinating lecture. "The audience followed the lecturer with deepest interest, as, with the aid of well selected lantern slides, he brought before them the salient features of that holy life," the journal reported.

All the national newspapers – and local ones, too – carried thanksgiving messages to Thérèse from readers for "favours received" or "petitions granted." They referred to graces obtained, including gratitude for a "successful operation and rapid recovery," "money received," "restoration to health" and numerous other benefits.

Among the messages was one Cork woman's thanksgiving for the "successful pass of my son at an examination" – she was careful to thank many intercessors, including Our Lady of Graces, the Blessed Virgin, St. Joseph, St. Colette, Little Nellie, and not just the Little Flower! Yet another thanked Thérèse – and also St. Anthony – "for finding Muff," who was presumably her beloved dog.

Given the new interest in Thérèse – and devotion to her, as well – *Story of a Soul* became a publishing sensation not only in Ireland but throughout the world. It was soon available in Italian, Spanish, Portuguese, Dutch and Polish; eventually, the book would find its way into all corners of the globe. The 1912 translation ended up being printed in almost 100 editions and being held in many thousands of libraries.

There was probably no surprise at its success. Although it was undoubtedly a profound and accessible insight to the nature of faith, it was more than that. It was also an extraordinary insight to the world of a young nun, a member of an austere order, hidden from view, and engaged in prayer and mortification. That alone made it a fascinating read.

There was also a lot to learn from the book. As one newspaper critic observed: "It is the old story of simplicity in God's service, of the perfect accomplishment of small recurring duties." Humility, self-effacement, obedience, unfaltering charity, with all the self-control and constant effort that they imply, were "written on every page." It was, the critic concluded, a "fitting bouquet" to the life of Thérèse of Lisieux.

The first media coverage of a pilgrimage to Lisieux appeared in Ireland in 1912. The article included an interview with Thérèse's sister, Pauline.

In 1912 – just 15 years after the death of the Little Flower – the influential Catholic journal, *Ave Maria*, turned its attention to recent happenings in Lisieux. Published out of the USA but popular in Ireland, the journal styled itself as a religious magazine for Catholic families. It was run by the Holy Cross Fathers – founders of Notre Dame, the "Irish" university in Indiana. The order would eventually become known for its "Rosary Priest", the Mayo-born Fr. Peyton.

By the early twentieth century, *Ave Maria* had developed many Irish connections including the frequent use of Irish authors. Among them were Dubliner Katharine Tynan, who was a close associate of W. B. Yeats, Waterford-born William Henry Grattan Flood, who was one of the most controversial Irish writers, composers and musicologists of his time, and Kildare-born Teresa Brayton, a writer and poet closely associated with the 1916 Rising.

In early autumn 1912, the journal asked yet another of its contributors – the French author Countess de Courson – to undertake a pilgrimage to Lisieux. Eventually containing a rare interview with Thérèse's sister Pauline, who was prioress at the Carmelite convent, it was no surprise that the resulting October edition of *Ave Maria* not only sold like hot cakes in Ireland, but the resulting article ended up being reprinted in *The Cork Examiner* in February 1913.

The first port of call for the author was the cemetery in Lisieux, where the body of Thérèse had been buried in the Carmelite enclosure. "It lies far above the town, and is reached by a country road, shaded by overhanging trees," the countess wrote. "When we lately visited the now hallowed spot, heavy rain had for weeks deluged the fertile Norman pastures; but on that particular afternoon the sun shone brightly through the clouds.

"On the open platform on which lies the city of the dead, the pilgrim gets an impression of light, sun, brightness, and peace. The town of Lisieux is so completely hidden by the rising ground that one might be miles away in the heart of the country; nothing strikes the eye but green fields and wooded hills. Little Thérèse, who enthusiastically loved the beauties of nature, is enshrined in surroundings after her own heart."

The author, at first, had difficulty finding the grave. Directions provided by the cemetery supervisor proved of little use. Soon, she was drawn by the low muttering sound of the rosary which, it turned out, was being recited aloud by a group of nuns praying by the white cross marking Thérèse's resting place. A further blast of white – white flowers, brought by pilgrims – covered the grave.

The author continued: "Other pilgrims – a priest, some poor women, a little child – were kneeling where the previous day had knelt a royal princess, the Countess d'Eu, hereditary Empress of Brazil. A few days before, three missionary bishops from Africa and one from Australia were among the pilgrims. Thus every day, at all seasons of the year, la petite Thérèse holds her court. Her clients come from the four quarters of the globe."

Surrounding Thérèse's grave were crosses marking the resting places of other Carmelite nuns. Among them was the grave of a nun whose death was predicted by the Little Flower. "The wooden cross that was formerly planted on the latter's grave was so mercilessly notched and cut away by relic-hunting pilgrims that it has now been replaced by an iron cross, painted white, which is safe from their indiscreet zeal," the article noted.

The countess and her companions eventually left the graveyard and began the long walk down the steep hill, along the quiet country roads, back to the Carmelite convent. "The convent at Lisieux," she wrote, "is naturally the centre of the extraordinary devotion that has sprung up towards the young sister, who more than once repeated on her deathbed the words that are inscribed on her grave: 'I wish to spend my time in heaven in doing good upon earth.' These words are being realised throughout the whole world.

"Over a hundred letters, begging for prayers, or thanking for favours obtained, are daily received at the convent; and, in consequence of the growing influx of pilgrims, the prioress, who, as already stated, is Thérèse's oldest sister, is obliged to decline to receive visitors." In the case of the countess, an exception was made and an interview granted.

"Behind the grille and curtain we heard the prioress tell of the little sister's sweetness, simplicity, kindness of heart, and overpowering love of God," the author recalled. "These things are written in her Life (Thérèse's book) and have often been read by her clients, but they gather fresh strength and meaning when spoken by those who shared her life and who knew her best.

"We asked the prioress if, in spite of the knowledge of her young sister's holiness, she had not been surprised at this sudden springing into fame of one so young, whose life was, apparently, hidden away from the sight of men. 'Yes,' she replied; 'I little thought she would make so much noise.' And we could feel that she smiled as she said the words."

The article also provided insights to the views of Thérèse's former companions in the convent, who had lived alongside the future saint. "Most of the religious who were her companions are still alive," the countess remarked. "They recognise that, in spite of constant endeavours to be ignored or forgotten, and in spite, too, of her great simplicity, she gave them the impression of being closely united to God and singularly favoured by Him.

"Her unfailing practice of trusting all things, spiritual and temporal, to her 'only Friend,' her readiness to oblige and serve others, her eagerness to do always what was hardest and most trying, her courage with withstanding terrible temptations against faith – all these things were veiled under a smiling exterior. There was nothing apparently extraordinary about her except the perfection of every action and the childlike confidence with which, whatever happened, she blessed and thanked God."

At the interview's conclusion, the Countess de Courson departed the Carmelite convent and returned home. There she wrote her article, which created such a stir when eventually published and distributed in Ireland and worldwide. Her final impressions, she wrote, were unequivocal and clear: Thérèse was "sweetly natural, simple, and humble; kind to others, eager to help them, and asking no return. There never was any touch of excitement about her, and no morbid self-examination, only a generous, absolute surrender to what best pleased God." It would be hard to come across a more favourable assessment than that.

News arriving in Ireland during 1912 of the conversion of a Presbyterian minister to Catholicism, thanks to Thérèse, generated enormous interest countrywide.

A pre-World War I visitor to Normandy might have been surprised if they called to the Little Flower's first home. Having knocked on the door of 42 Rue St. Blaise, Alençon – which in Thérèse's time was numbered 36 – it would have been answered by a person with a strange intonation to their voice. In place of a flowery French accent, the visitor would have been greeted by a noticeable Scottish burr.

If the visitor happened to be from Ireland, they would have been even more surprised if the owners introduced themselves by name. The penny might have dropped if they heard they were Rev. Alexander Grant and his wife Ethel Grant. In recent times, their names had been splashed across newspaper headlines back home. Whether you came from Derry or Cork, you most likely knew of the Grants.

The Grants' story was a fascinating one, involving soul-searching, mental anguish and persecution in their native Scotland. Their sorry tale, with a happy ending, had begun on the Isle of Arran, with its tall, windswept mountains, picturesque villages and beautiful shores. It was there, in the first decade of the twentieth century, that a minister of the United Free Church of Scotland – a branch of the Presbyterian Church – by the name of Rev. Grant cared for his flock.

All went well until his wife, Ethel, decided to convert to Catholicism. Her husband's position became difficult, to put it mildly. It didn't go down well that on Sundays Rev. Grant would conduct his Presbyterian services while his wife assisted at Mass in the Catholic chapel. As the local newspaper, the *Campbeltown Courier*, put it, there was "so much hostility among the islanders" that it was realised that Rev. Grant's ministry "could not be continued."

The minister's flock came up with an extraordinary proposal, designed to resolve the dilemma. "The ultimatum of the people, freely expressed at the time, amounted to this, that if Mr. Grant separated from his wife the old relations of minister and people would be resumed," the local newspaper reported. This draconian measure was rejected outright by the couple, who were, instead, forced to leave Arran and move from place to place. In effect, Rev. Grant became a missionary minister, at least for a time.

By all accounts, it seems that Rev. Grant refrained from persuading his wife to return to her original faith. In turn, Ethel never overtly tried to persuade her husband to become a Catholic. She did put little temptations in his way, especially in the form of a picture of the Little Flower which she placed in his study. She also prayed to Thérèse in the hope of securing his conversion. We additionally know that, at some stage, Rev. Grant got his hands on the Little Flower's autobiography and was overwhelmed by what he read.

Having devoured *Story of a Soul* from cover to cover, he later remarked in a letter to Mother Agnès – Thérèse's sister, Pauline – at the Carmel in Lisieux: "I found there had fallen into my hands the work of a genius as well as of a theologian and poet of the first order....The impression proved as lasting as it was extraordinary."

Reading the book proved to be the turning point in Rev. Grant's life. The influence of Thérèse, he said, "awakened in me a genuine interest in the whole question of Catholicism, setting me to the study of it with an open mind and with no little seriousness." The key difficulty was battling lifelong prejudices which he said he had developed through his Presbyterian beliefs. Although he had previously "dipped into Catholic books," it was not "with the object of discovering the exact nature of its teaching, but only to find matter for arguments against it," he reflected.

Having read Thérèse's book, Rev. Grant ended up with a completely different perspective and developed an enormous admiration for the future saint. "I almost worshipped her; she seemed to me so amiable, so beautiful," he revealed. He also decided that Catholicism was the religion for him. "The result was that at last the light of conviction dawned," the minister concluded.

Rev. Alexander Grant was received into the Catholic Church on 20 April 1911. The news created quite a stir in the press. "United Free Church Loses a Minister Who Joins the Catholic Fold" was the headline in *The Irish News and Belfast Morning News*. "A Notable Conversion" headlined *The Derry Journal* and *The Cork Examiner*. "No small triumph for the Little Flower that she should open the eyes of a member of the United Free ministry," another commentator wrote. "Mr. Grant is far from young, and is also a scholar, circumstances which enhance her victory," he added.

At the time of his conversion, Rev. Grant was residing in Edinburgh, and he remained there for some time. We might never have known what happened to him after that but for a few brief references – indirect though they were – in a number of publications. One of those references came from an Irish-American priest who happened to knock on the door of 42 Rue St. Blaise, Alençon, and was surprised by the person answering the door.

"I rang the bell, and the door was opened by Madame Grant, the wife of the Rev. Mr. Grant," Fr. Bernard J. Quinn later wrote. "Needless to say, when I told her that I was an American priest, she welcomed me most cordially. I stopped there that night, and on the following morning, the Little Flower's birthday, I had the supreme pleasure of offering the Holy Sacrifice of the Mass in the room where she was born. I speak of this as a very great privilege, because I was the first priest to say Mass there."

Fr. Quinn paid many subsequent visits to Thérèse's home, sleeping in a bedroom next to the one in which she was born and reading his breviary in the garden where she had played as a child. Those visits were happy ones, he said: "Many were the evenings that I sat by the fireside of the little dining room, and listened to Madame Grant speak so lovingly of the Little Flower. She knew her life so intimately. I regret now that I did not put down in writing the many things she told me."

You may have noted that no mention has been made so far of Rev. Grant's presence in the modest two-storey home of Thérèse. The reason is simple – by the time of Fr. Quinn's visits, Rev. Grant had passed away. He had realised his wish of living in the Little Flower's first home and, after his death, was buried in the same graveyard where the future saint had been laid to rest.

"But for her I should still be an unhappy Protestant wandering in the night," Rev. Grant had once said of Thérèse. "But for her I should never have lent an ear to Catholic truth, and never have considered it deserving of the trouble of inquiry. It was she who won my heart to its study, and sustained my interest in it till at last I entered the one true fold of the Great Shepherd of the sheep."

A remarkable County Donegal miracle, occurring in 1913, was attributed to the Little Flower.

Arctic weather conditions were experienced in Donegal during the winter months of 1912 – 1913. Heavy snow fell on the county, blocking mountain roads and making travel hazardous. Lakes froze to a depth of several inches. All outdoor work was suspended, and Saturday markets were poorly attended owing to the depth of snow on the roads.

Things didn't ease up in the week preceding Christmas. Thunderstorms, with lightning and hail, battered shoppers as they went about their festive chores. Vicious gales followed in January, causing damage on land and sea. Older people complained that they couldn't remember such prolonged bad weather, especially as it followed a wet summer. "But what is the use of complaining?" they said. It was just one of those years.

It certainly wasn't the weather for snowdrops to put in an early appearance. They were still sleeping, waiting for brighter, warmer days to come in late winter and early spring. Only then would they show their faces, revealing beautiful white petals after a wintry sleep. There was one exception, however, when a strange bunch of snowdrops entered the home of a Donegal family– an event that changed their lives forever.

The family in question lived in a townland on the road from Glenties to the small seaside village of Narin, in the parish of Ardara. The area was – and still is – a beautiful one, situated north-west of the Bluestack Mountains, where two glens meet. On 27 January, trouble entered the family's lives. It came in the form of life-threatening medical complications following the birth of their latest child, Mary Frances Teresa McNelis.

The mother – also called Mary – had developed puerperal fever, an infection that occasionally arises after childbirth. In those pre-antibiotic days, contracting the infection was bad enough, but when it developed into septicaemia, or blood poisoning, it was often fatal. Things certainly seemed to be moving in that direction for Mrs. McNelis, resulting, at 2 am on Monday, 27 January 1913, in doctors being summoned to her bedside. A priest was called, too, and he believed the end was near.

As devotees of the Little Flower, the family prayed for her help and intercession. They knew that she was busy and in high demand, having learned about her popularity from newspapers and by word of mouth. As a result, on more than one occasion, they remarked: "She is so busy, I wonder if she will think of poor Donegal!" They needed her, and they needed her now, right here at their family home.

Later that morning, around 11 o'clock, the family's four-year-old child, Kathleen, arrived in the house with a beautiful bunch of snowdrops in her hand. Her father noted that there were six in all. She told her father, Michael, that they had been given to her by a nun, who said they were for her mother and she would be cured. Given that the child was only four years old, and there were no nuns in the area – no snowdrops, either – it was understandable that the incident was dismissed for the time being.

That changed, however, when a sweet perfume pervaded the house, filling not only the room containing the flowers but every corner of the family home. All present were puzzled, wondering about the source of the aroma. Having identified it, they then wondered where snowdrops had come from at that time of the year, and how their perfume was so pronounced.

They turned once more to the little child, asking her what had happened. She explained how a nun had come down from on high and handed her the bunch of flowers, adding that she should pass them on along with the message regarding how her mother would become well. The nun, she said, was beautiful and wore white, and she disappeared as quickly as she came.

Almost instantly, Mary McNelis recovered, surprising all concerned. Not only had she survived a potentially-fatal illness, but one of the doctors later noted that her health became better than in the previous two years. Everyone was overjoyed, no doubt including the daughter Kathleen, who eventually grew up, got married and died in Dublin in 2001, after "a long and inspirational life," according to her death notice.

As for the snowdrops, they continued to fill the house with their perfume for the rest of the week. A doctor who had attended Mrs. McNelis took two of them with him to a friend who was also experiencing serious medical issues, and the scent pervaded that person's house, too. The whole thing left the family believing the child's story of the nun. The Little Flower had, after all, remembered Donegal. "What a gracious way she has of doing good upon earth," the father concluded.

An Irish priest, who made a pilgrimage to Lisieux in 1914, wrote about the visit on his return. He gave a particularly graphic account of the grave of Thérèse, among other places in the town.

The official supplier of Thérèse souvenirs in Lisieux, in 1914, was located on the Rue de Livarot, close to the Carmel. It was a wonderful shop, full of books and brochures, postcards, notepaper, copybooks and other bric-a-brac, all stacked on the shelves. There were portraits and prayer cards of Thérèse painted and designed by her sister, the talented Céline.

For visitors from Ireland entering the shop, the biggest surprise was that the *madame la dispensatrice* – the shopkeeper – was Irish. According to one visitor who encountered her in 1914, she was charming, distinguished and spoke French like a native. She also was the only English-speaking resident in Lisieux.

A Dubliner, she had come to Lisieux following a miraculous cure received by her sister. "My sister was given up for death by three doctors, who said she had but a few minutes to live," the woman explained. "I made a vow to the Little Flower that if my dying sister were cured, I would devote the rest of my life in spreading devotion to her benefactress. My sister was cured instantly; and here I am." It was obvious to the visitor that the Dublin woman was wholeheartedly devoted to her "dear little Thérèse."

The visitor in question was the Kilkenny-born priest, Rev. J. A. Dowling, who had embarked on a personal pilgrimage to

Lisieux on the eve of World War I. Fr. Dowling came from a well-known religious family and was a cousin of Most Rev. Dr. John Pius Dowling, Archbishop of Port of Spain, Trinidad. He wrote extensively and served in many parishes, among them parishes in Waterford, Newry and Drogheda. In Waterford, he was described as a "zealous priest" and a "general favourite" who had "endeared himself to all."

Fr. Dowling's itinerary in Lisieux was ambitious, with visits planned to Les Buissonnets, the Carmel, the Church of St. Pierre, the Benedictine Abbey and, above all, the resting place of the Little Flower in the municipal cemetery. Yet here he was, on the morning of day one, entering his first port of call, the shop at No. 46 Rue de Livarot, and bumping into a woman from home.

"Here in this modest little shop she does a brisk business, and sends her pious wares to all parts of the world," Fr. Dowling later remarked in an article featured in *The Catholic Bulletin*, a monthly review published out of Dublin. "In the *procure* (the shop) is an imposing display of attractions for the clients of the Servant of God. Everything relating to her is here, and everything, of course, is of the best....The visitor to the *procure* will come away with a very high opinion of our charming countrywoman."

Of Fr. Dowling's many destinations, it was the grave of Thérèse that stood out; it was also the location he described best in his report. He walked the half-hour's journey from his *maison de famille* – a family guesthouse, popular with priests – to the cemetery on the outskirts of town. Climbing the steep hill to the burial ground, he was enchanted by the wonderful vista of the valley below.

"Before you come to the Carmelite enclosure, midway between it and the grand entrance, a tomb on the left cannot fail to attract your attention," Fr. Dowling observed. "It is that of the Martin family. Here, awaiting a glorious resurrection, lie the remains of the father and mother of the *thaumaturge* (miracle worker), her grandparents, and her four little brothers and sisters who died in infancy."

Fr. Dowling found the Carmelite enclosure located nearby and was directed to the spot where Thérèse's body had been buried for 13 years. The body had been exhumed in 1910. "When the coffin was placed on the trestles, the shock caused the bones to fall apart," the priest remarked. He then moved to her new burial place, where she was reinterred in a grave lined with bricks.

"The grave is almost smothered in flowers," he noted. "On the modest cross, around the flowery grille, grateful hands have placed *ex-votos* (offerings of gratitude or devotion) of various kinds – chaplets, ribands, medals, bundles of letters, visiting-cards. One cannot help seeing, too, suppliant appeals addressed to the Servant of God scribbled in French on the porcelain leaves and roses. A notice on the iron railing surrounding the plot prohibits the lighting of candles and the depositing of money and costly offerings on the grave."

During the year preceding Fr. Dowling's visit, some 60,000 people had travelled from all parts of the world to pray at Thérèse's grave. On the day he arrived, in 1914, people were there, too: "Some half-a-dozen pilgrims in their feast-day finery were prostrate before the tomb telling their beads. In the midst of the motley group, a soldier, all colour and glitter, made a bright point of interest in the afternoon greyness.

"One could see at a glance that these pilgrims were animated by something better than mere curiosity. There was an unmistakable *cachet* of deep earnestness over them; and one was led irresistibly to the conclusion that Soeur Thérèse is most passionately dear to these silent, solemn people, and that they almost feel her spirit hovering about its forsaken shrine, and conscious of the very thoughts they cherish."

In the years ahead, the number of people visiting Lisieux skyrocketed, with more than half a million arriving annually by the late 1920s. They came for many reasons, as Fr. Dowling explained in his fine article in *The Catholic Bulletin*: "The ill and the well, the whole and the infirm throng the steep road leading to the cemetery, devoutly reciting the rosary. Men and women whose bodies ache with the infinite pains of disease; whose hearts ache with the infinite woes of the world; whose souls ache with the infinite burden of guilt – all come here and find relief and consolation."

The results are abundantly apparent, he said – the "countless conversions," the "inextricable difficulties she has unravelled," the "celestial gifts" she has scattered in "grand and almost reckless profusion," and the miracles which have been "the rule not the exception." He concluded: "This new Glory of Carmel" has "taken the world by storm, and comforted the souls of thousands of human beings."

Little Flower Penny Dinners was established in 1912 to feed the hungry in the Liberties area of Dublin. It was inspired by Thérèse of Lisieux.

In 1826, a newly-qualified Dublin doctor, Dr. Dominic Corrigan, had a revelation regarding the grinding poverty in the city.

What was the point, he wondered, in providing medical relief to the poor when they were consumed by hunger? He took matters in his capable hands. Through the Sick Poor Institution, in Meath Street, in the Liberties area of the city, he initiated a campaign to make food available to the hungry and for hot meals to be distributed to those who couldn't afford the price of coal.

Jump forward to the dawn of the twentieth century, and nothing had changed in Dublin. In fact, things had got worse. By 1912, tens of thousands of families were crowded into filthy, rat-infested, disease-ridden tenements, which were full of starving adults and children. Twenty thousand families lived in one-room hovels. The city claimed the dubious distinction of having the worst housing conditions in the British Isles.

With the arrival around that time of the first newspaper coverage concerning Thérèse, someone had a bright idea. Once again, it was conceived in Meath Street. Why not, it was proposed, offer penny dinners to the hungry and do so under her protection and guidance? Titled Little Flower Penny Dinners, it provided two million hot meals, in the next nine years, to destitute men, women and children. It continues to do so today, well over a century later.

Although receiving almost no general publicity – certainly in terms of features in the national press – the work of Little Flower Penny Dinners was phenomenal from its inception. In one November fortnight, during World War I, it provided the poor with 550 free breakfasts, almost 3,000 cooked meals and over 5,500 children's meals. Six gallons of milk were distributed in one day alone.

In subsequent years, while still receiving little media coverage, the centre mustered support from the general public partly by appeals in the advertising columns of newspapers, seeking donations to keep its work going. It also issued regular radio appeals, using the hugely-popular wireless technology of the era to great effect.

Just as the centre needed money, the poor needed food. "For one penny" the poor "can get a plate of Irish stew and for another penny, tea, bread and butter," Fr. J. Meagher said in a 1957 radio appeal on behalf of the centre. He remarked that Little Flower Penny Dinners provided not only "a comfortable dining hall" but also "a well-heated shelter where the poor people may rest until they start to eat." In these "cold and jobless days," he added, "the number of the poor was increasing, and everything possible was done for them at the Little Flower Dining Hall."

Early support for the centre was bolstered by the fear among Catholics that "proselytisers" or "evangelists" were infiltrating the city and converting the faithful. One letter writer to *The Freeman's Journal* – "a Dublin priest", he called himself – wrote of the "vile traffic in human souls." He singled out the Coombe – also in the Liberties – as "a happy hunting ground." He also praised the dining rooms and breakfasts of the relatively new centre.

Another report – once again in *The Freeman's Journal* – heartily endorsed the provision of "breakfasts to poor destitute Catholic children," thereby putting a stop to "the great evil of proselytising that is such a menace to the faith of the very poor who live in the slums of our city." Prevention is better than cure, the article concluded, arguing that "by providing breakfasts on

Sundays under Catholic management the destitute children of the district need no longer have recourse to the local Mission Halls."

It is not known whether the pioneering founders of Little Flower Penny Dinners were aware of Thérèse's concern for the poor. Had they read *Story of a Soul*, they certainly would have been clued in. In the book, she related how she frequently gave alms to those she encountered on her Sunday walks. She singled out a story of how, one day, when she was six years old, she came across a poor old man dragging himself along on crutches.

"I went up to give him a penny," she recalled. "He looked sadly at me for a long time, and then, shaking his head with a sorrowful smile, he refused my alms. I cannot tell you what I felt; I had wished to help and comfort him, and instead of that, I had, perhaps, hurt him and caused him pain. He must have guessed my thought, for I saw him turn round and smile at me when we were some way off.

"Just then Papa bought me a cake. I wished very much to run after the old man and give it to him, for I thought: 'Well, he did not want money, but I am sure he would like to have a cake.' I do not know what held me back, and I felt so sad I could hardly keep from crying.

"Then I remembered having heard that one obtains all the favours asked for on one's First Communion Day. This thought consoled me immediately, and though I was only six years old at the time, I said to myself: 'I will pray for my poor old man on the day of my First Communion.' Five years later I faithfully kept my resolution."

Thérèse's concern for the poor and her deep compassion for the needy were enshrined in the work of Little Flower Penny

Dinners from its foundation in 1912. Many may find it hard to credit that a centre established before the 1913 Lockout, the 1916 Rising and two world wars should still be in business today. But it is. Perhaps it is part of that "shower of roses" Thérèse promised such a long time ago.

Ireland's first escorted tour to the grave of St. Thérèse left Dublin on the eve of World War I. The journey was an arduous one by any standards.

At 9.20 pm, on Tuesday, 12 May 1914, the first package tour carrying Irish people to Lisieux departed from the North Wall quay in Dublin. There was a long journey ahead – by boat to Britain, train to London, then across the channel to France and onward to the grave of the Little Flower via Dieppe and Rouen. Helped on by west to north-west winds, the weather was fresh, sea conditions fair and the temperature below normal as the steamer sailed out into Dublin Bay.

The passengers – or pilgrims, for that's what they were – were heading to a tense, uneasy, agitated country which would shortly become one of the killing fields of Europe. Just over two months after the tour departed, World War I would erupt, with most of its battles being waged on the Franco-German borders. There was better news, however – around the time of departure, the first steps were being taken by Pope Pius X which would eventually lead to the beatification of the Little Flower.

Organised by Hewett's Travel Agency, D'Olier Street, Dublin – and escorted by the company's owner Albert William Hewett – the full package, covering eight days, cost 7 ½ guineas. After a long career in the travel business – having been initially employed by the esteemed Gaze & Sons agency of Dublin's

Suffolk Street – there could hardly have been a better tour organiser than Mr. Hewett. Unfortunately, while this would be his company's first organised trip to Lisieux, it would also be its last. The war would see to that.

Unaffected, as yet, by the horrors of warfare, the town of Lisieux in May 1914 was undergoing radical transformation caused in no small part by extraordinary happenings that had taken place in the Carmelite convent a few decades earlier. From the moment of their arrival, the pilgrims no doubt noted the new apartment houses juxtaposed with old Roman ruins, historic timbered dwellings and ancient buildings nodding at each other across the town's streets. The water supply, on the other hand, as one commentator put it, "is so frequently contaminated with matters of non-hygienic value, to say the least, that it often assumes a more or less dark hue."

The hustle and bustle of the railway station painted a more refreshing picture for the Irish contingent, crammed as it was in 1914 with travellers arriving to visit the grave of the future saint. As one travel writer noted, the Great Western Railroad, which ran the local train network, would likely have compensated for its well-known annual deficit by the new business that had miraculously sprung up. "What has happened?" the travel writer asked. "Apparently nothing, or next to that," he replied rhetorically. Well, there is one thing, he suddenly remembered – "At Lisieux there is a Carmel."

The "Carmel", of course, referred to the monastery run by the Carmelites of Lisieux since 1838. The impressive building presented a fine spectacle to the visiting Irish pilgrims. It was here, behind cloistered walls, that Thérèse had lived her life of prayer, silence and solitude. It was here, too, that three of her sisters had lived alongside Thérèse. The Carmel, however, was of secondary interest to the tour members compared to the primary purpose of their visit – to attend at "the Grave of the Little Flower," as Hewett's advertising literature had put it.

Back in 1914, it took shoe leather, and some exertion, to walk from the Carmel to the municipal cemetery where the body of Thérèse was buried. There, pilgrims knelt by the grave, which was normally covered with white flowers. At the head of the grave stood a large cross covered in pilgrims' writings and bearing the self-explanatory inscription, "Sr. Thérèse De L'Enfant Jesus." Beneath it was a smaller-sized inscription, also in French, which translated into Thérèse's famous saying, "I will spend my heaven doing good on earth."

That grave which the Irish tour visited in 1914 was, in fact, the second plot to have been occupied by Thérèse's remains since her death in 1897. She had been exhumed from her initial nearby resting place in 1910 once inquiries began into her sanctity, constituting the first step on the road to canonisation. As Thérèse was reported to have predicted in a visionary appearance to a fellow sister at that time, only her bones would be found, and that is exactly what happened. A palm branch placed in her hand after death had also survived. The gravediggers additionally detected the scent of violets from the casket.

No doubt enthralled by their visit, the Hewett's tour party eventually began their long journey home, retracing the outward trip – travelling second class – from Lisieux back to London, and then on by rail and boat to Ireland, arriving in the early hours of the morning at Dublin's North Wall. There would be no more tours for the duration of the war, nor would Hewett's ever enter the Lisieux market again. Instead, the company would be displaced by other tour operators including the Catholic Travel Association and a Le Havre-based Irish company, Keating, offering new-fangled "motor car travel" all the way to the future saint's grave.

It wasn't that Albert William Hewett left the travel business; in fact, his company thrived for many years to come. Other continental destinations, including Lourdes, along with places like New York, dominated his tour schedules. Hewett also became a respected member of the Dublin business community, being recognised for his contributions to the Dublin Rotary Club, the Companions of St. Patrick – fostering "goodwill among Irishmen" – and the Society of St. George, a patriotic society encouraging interest in the English way of life. Regarding this latter interest, it must be noted that he had been born in Sussex, was a member of the Anglican Church, and was married to an English woman.

In March 1939, Albert William Hewett died at his home in Sandycove, Dublin. Newspaper readers must have been very impressed by the list of mourners at his funeral. They included the Lord Mayor of Dublin, Alfie Byrne T.D., together with leading representatives from the many societies he had joined, along with senior officials from the Cunard White Star Line, United States Lines, American Express, Limerick Steamship Co. and various travel agencies.

No doubt, his passing was also noted by those who were fortunate enough to have travelled with him in 1914. Not only was it Ireland's first formal package tour to the grave of St. Thérèse, but it set in train a steady flow of Irish pilgrims to Lisieux and a national obsession with the Little Flower that persists to this day.

The final story in this chapter concerns a priest from Sligo, a businessman from Bangor, in County Down, and a miracle attributed to Thérèse of Lisieux. The events occurred on the eve of the Great War.

In August 1914, at the start of World War I, a priest based in Sevenoaks, Kent, published the first complete study of Thérèse's life. The book received some complimentary reviews. The *Irish Independent* praised it as a "beautiful book" and commended its author for his "fine literary style." The newspaper went further, stating that it "should find an honoured place in every Catholic home."

Unfortunately, *The Unfolding of the Little Flower* disappeared without trace and its author faded from view. Fr. William M. Cunningham, who wrote it, was, according to the publishers, rector of the Church of Saint Thomas the Martyr, Sevenoaks, Kent. He was also, they said, Vicar Forane for the County of Kent – a supervisory Church role involving the overseeing of clerical discipline, among other duties. There the trail ended – Fr. Cunningham wrote no further books of note; there was nothing more to report.

Subsequent research, involving newspaper archives, census documents, and birth and death records, revealed that Fr. Cunningham had been born in Sligo town in 1863 – at a time when the Civil War raged in America and the Famine in Ireland had only recently concluded. Eventually joining the priesthood, he ended up in Britain and was instrumental in building the Church of St. Thomas, in Sevenoaks, where he was rector for

20 years. He also travelled extensively in Normandy, becoming one of the earliest devotees of Thérèse.

It was that devotion to the Little Flower – "a living example of sanctity," he called her – that prompted the publication of his book. It also led him to become acquainted with stories of various miracles and cures. Among them was a case history related by James Murray, another resident of Sevenoaks. Replicating Fr. Cunningham's relative anonymity, Mr. Murray's background also remained obscure – other than a reference in the book that his father lived in Bangor, County Down.

Later research revealed that James Murray was also Irish-born, entering the world in 1856. Eventually, he moved to England, where he worked as a shipbroker with a company of foreign carriers called Riley's. He was a bachelor and became a principal partner with the company. As a resident of Sevenoaks, he knew Fr. Cunningham. Through that connection the story of Thérèse's miraculous cure came to light.

In April 1914, James Murray received an urgent message that his father, who was aged 95 and living in Bangor, was critically ill and had no hope of survival. His doctor informed the family to return home and say their final farewells. Before departing, James asked Fr. Cunningham to pray for his father's happy death. This the priest did, with his appeal being directed to the intercession of Thérèse. Unknown to Murray, his sister – who was also a devotee of Thérèse – was praying to her, too.

After the various appeals to the Little Flower, it appears that the father had a remarkable recovery. By the time James arrived in Bangor, he had completely revived. Despite his age, and the grave prognosis, he had returned to rude good health.

Fr. Cunningham later wrote in his book: "Without any warning their father suddenly announced his intention one morning of getting up and coming down to breakfast. To their astonishment he dressed without difficulty, went down stairs and refusing all invalid diet, made a hearty breakfast of bacon and eggs.

"Within a couple of weeks Mr. Murray was back again at his business in London, and was able to tell his friends, some of whom had begun consoling with him, that when he left Bangor the day before, his father was busy mowing the lawn.

"A subsequent letter received by him on May 13th, 1914, conveyed the cheering assurance that his father had so completely recovered that he was once more thoroughly enjoying himself, in his 96th year, digging in the garden."

On his return to London, James Murray contacted a friend in France and informed him of his father's remarkable revival. The reply – which arrived by return of post – recounted a further instance of recovery. This time it concerned the friend's elderly father, who was 90 years of age.

It seems that the father was at death's door, having suffered from bronchitis and congestion of the lungs, followed a few days later by phlebitis. "He remained ill for so long that on Thursday last we felt convinced that his last hour was at hand," the letter writer said.

All hope was lost, and the man's father was given the last sacraments. Fearing death was imminent, the family placed around his neck a relic of the Little Flower and, as the friend remarked, "made certain promises to be carried out by us in the event of our father being saved."

The improvement was immediate. "When the doctor called the next morning there was scarcely any trace left of his phlebitis," according to the friend. Since then, he made steady progress towards recovery, surprising both the doctor and the man's family. "I only hope his convalescence will not be too lengthy" was the man's final remark.

There are some interesting and unfortunate postscripts to this story. James Murray, having returned to London, remained there for only a short time. He soon came back to Ireland. It may have been to care for his ageing father or, as records reveal, it may have been because he developed tuberculosis. We know of his illness because, the following year – in August 1915 – he died in Bangor from a combination of TB and diabetes.

By a strange irony, his father outlived him. So, also, did Fr. Cunningham. The priest remained in Sevenoaks until 1916, after which he changed parish and survived to the ripe age of 72. He died in Bromley, Kent, in 1935, no doubt recalling Thérèse's miracles and cures which, as he put it, brought "relief and comfort to her brethren in every corner of the wide earth."

THE ANGEL OF THE TRENCHES

It wasn't for nothing that Thérèse of Lisieux became known as The Angel of the Trenches. In the face of death, during World War I, soldiers on all sides turned to her for protection and support. They prayed to her as they marched into battle, and they prayed to her as they lay in their trenches while under enemy fire.

She is said to have appeared on 40 occasions on various battlefields, caring for the injured, attending to the dead and calming the nerves of soldiers who could take no more. She became the patroness of the Allies and their enemies, "the shield of soldiers", "the little sister of the trenches", the person everyone turned to when bullets flew and cannons roared.

Many believe that the renown she acquired during the war was responsible for her later elevation to sainthood. How she achieved that renown is illustrated in the following stories, depicting extraordinary miracles, strange apparitions and other accounts from the battlefields of Europe.

Religious medals and prayer cards depicting Thérèse of Lisieux became popular with soldiers on all sides of the conflict during World War I. Mass attendance and other forms of devotion grew rapidly, too.

Prayer cards featuring photographs of Thérèse were in high demand during the war. Soldiers travelled by train to secure supplies from the Carmel at Lisieux. Money was posted in envelopes asking the nuns to send them to the front. Everyone wanted to have one in their wallet or breast pocket, keeping it close to their heart as protection.

The cards were particularly poignant, featuring the innocent face of Thérèse. She seemed kind and compassionate. She was also young, just like the soldiers themselves. More importantly, they were aware of the suffering and sacrifice she had endured, not unlike their daily hell in the trenches.

The troops also cried out for medals. Like the prayer cards, they acquired them from the Carmel in Lisieux. They wore the medals around their necks or kept them in their pockets, believing they would act as a safeguard. This they sometimes did, with soldiers reporting how bullets ricocheted off the medals and saved them from death.

Bowing to the pressure for relics, the Vatican amended its rule forbidding the striking of a medal for anyone who was not beatified or canonised, and using it for the purpose of devotion and prayer. Not only did Pope Benedict XV allow an exception in the case of Thérèse, but he took an active role in supervising the medal's design and the choice of inscription used.

"This extraordinary privilege will be a great consolation to clients of the Little Flower," one commentator wrote of the Vatican's initiative, "and will be especially consoling to those who are defending their country amidst the untold perils which surround them in the great conflict which is now laying waste the fair fields of Europe."

Understandably, in the trenches, praying to Thérèse and to the saints was the order of the day. Organising and attending Masses was important, too. One County Monaghan soldier wrote to his mother describing how he and his colleagues had arranged with a priest to have Masses said for their dead companions. "We scraped together what odd money we had," he wrote, "but his reverence wouldn't hear of taking any money for prayers for the relief of the brave lads who had died so far from the old land."

Another soldier – this time from County Kerry – described in a letter how his battalion had a nice Catholic chaplain, an Englishman he believed. "When not in the trenches," he remarked, "we take every opportunity of going to Mass, and the priest gives absolution to all the soldiers by their kneeling down and saying an Act of Contrition. I have had an interview with him, as one never knows what is going to happen here."

The soldiers also sent letters to the Carmel in Lisieux. In them, they poured out their troubles and offered words of thanks. They described reciting prayers from Thérèse's cards, praying to her, talking to her and taking confidence from her in times of need. Some wrote of miracles. Almost all spoke of how she accompanied them in the trenches.

On the domestic front, the interest in Thérèse was equally intense. Personal messages in newspapers thanked her for favours received, many of them referring to news regarding family members fighting on the front. Advertisements appeared in the press offering novenas in return for a financial contribution; people who replied were promised "a beautiful illustrated memento leaflet for deceased soldiers or sailors" and a copy of "the pope's prayer for peace."

Poignant scenes depicting the departure of soldiers on their way to France were described in the Irish press. *The Cork Examiner* detailed one particularly moving event. "Yesterday," according to the newspaper, "there was witnessed one of those very affecting scenes at the G.S. and W.R. station, Cork, that have been very frequent since the war started."

Referring to the departure of soldiers on the 12.45 pm train, the newspaper outlined how priests had given them medals, badges and other religious emblems. The report added: "Then, just before the train started, the priests entered each carriage, said prayers appropriate to the occasion, and gave all present absolution. During the short service the men, with heads bared, stood to attention, and not a few of them were able to keep back tears of gratitude to the priests for their kindly ministrations."

The soldiers travelling from Cork were a mere fraction of the number of Irishmen who travelled to the battlefields of World War I. It is estimated that well over 200,000 served in the conflict, with over 35,000 of them perishing. Given the number of parents, wives and children they left behind, the spread of devotion in Ireland to Thérèse was no surprise.

This pattern was replicated abroad, resulting in one Irish newspaper commenting in 1916: "Nothing is more remarkable than the manner in which recognition of the sanctity of the Little Flower has spread in a materialistic age, even in the midst of a cruel and terrible war which inevitably engages all the energies of all the peoples involved. In every land the name of Little Thérèse has become, in very truth, a household word, and this not only among Catholics, but even among Protestants, many of whom recognise her holiness."

With popularity like that, it was inevitable that Thérèse would be made a saint, and that it would happen soon. Already, in 1910, the first moves had been made towards her canonisation.

By the end of the war, in 1918, her sanctity had been well-established – certainly in the eyes of the public – and in 1925 she would become a saint. In the meantime, there was still a war to be fought, battles to be won and miraculous events to occur, as the following stories reveal.

An Irish soldier had a miraculous near miss on the Western Front during World War I. He attributed his good fortune to Thérèse of Lisieux.

At break of dawn – around 4.30 am – Lance Corporal Francis Coyle was crouched in the trenches at Loos, in northern France. The region around Loos had seen bitter fighting in recent days. German forces had launched heavy artillery bombardments and gas attacks on the British trenches. Gallant defending had repulsed them. Like the rest of his fellow soldiers, Coyle was on high alert, fearing that another gas attack was imminent.

The Munster Fusiliers, who were in the trenches alongside Coyle's battalion, the 7th Leinsters, were also fearful of an imminent attack. They fired a rocket in the air – as an SOS – signalling for artillery assistance. Coyle braced himself, believing that the rocket might draw the attention of the Germans. He expected an instant response.

Coyle reached for his pocket, where he had a picture of the Little Flower. It had a short prayer on the reverse side. It was just one of many Little Flower cards he had procured, distributing them to his fellow soldiers, especially the Irish. He believed it was important to make her known among his comrades, particularly at a time of war. Anticipating the worst, he felt he badly needed her help, and he needed it now.

"Having a picture of the Little Flower in my pocket, it was my intention to say the prayer on the back of it, for I felt that death was coming," Coyle later recalled. "But there was no time for that. So I said: 'Soeur Thérèse, save us.' Instantly, a shell burst over our trench, threw my comrade on his head, and smashed rifles and Lewis gun and everything around, sandbags and all."

The comrade he referred to was another Irishman, Peter Robinson, from Portlaoise. Like many in the trenches, he was a young recruit. Coyle rushed over to help him. He tried to lift him, only to discover that the shell had wounded Robinson in the neck and wrist. He was clearly badly injured – he would die a few hours later.

Coyle took a clasp knife from his breast pocket to adjust a field dressing on his comrade. The breast pocket was positioned directly over his heart. To his amazement, he discovered that the two blades in the knife were knocked out and smashed. He also had a purse in the same pocket, containing nine pennies. Two of the pennies were completely twisted by shrapnel.

"I had not time to make a further search," Coyle recollected, instead calling for stretcher-bearers for his wounded fellow soldier. "Then I made a further examination, and found that my tunic was fairly riddled with shrapnel. I counted eleven holes, but, thanks and praises be to God and to the Little Flower, I was unhurt." He also found that his water bottle was twisted out of shape. Even some letters, which had been with the Little Flower picture in his pocket, were completely pierced through.

Soon, the two men – Coyle and Robinson – were joined by the regimental chaplain, another Irishman, a Jesuit by the name of Rafter. The chaplain brought Coyle to the doctor, saying to the medic: "Here is one absolutely riddled with shrapnel." He was also seen by his lieutenant – Belfast man, Lieutenant Cullen – who remarked that Coyle had had "a miraculous escape." Which, indeed, he had! "The shock of it all stayed with me for a long time," the lance corporal remarked.

Coyle's wartime link to Thérèse didn't end there. In 1918, he was with his regiment, travelling by train from Rouen to Trouville, when he noticed a sign saying "Lisieux" at a station they passed by. He inquired from a curate – another Irishman, Fr. O'Connor – if that was the home of the Little Flower. "Yes," the priest responded, "and I am going there on a pilgrimage tomorrow with twenty-five wounded soldiers." Coyle told him of his wartime miracle, and the priest responded that he already had 24 names lined up for the pilgrimage, adding: "Yours will be the twenty-fifth."

The following day, the pilgrimage set out for Lisieux. There, Lance Corporal Coyle was introduced to Mother Agnès, who was Thérèse's sister, Pauline. He told her his story and she was impressed with the account. No doubt wanting to give Coyle a memento of his visit, she handed him a letter as he was about to depart.

Written in French, the letter translates: "I ask my heavenly little sister to give you a great share of the shower of roses which she has promised to send down upon earth." It was signed by Mother Agnès and dated 4 November 1918, exactly a week before World War I formally came to a close.

Appearances by the Little Flower on the battlefields of Europe were reported during World War I. The following is one such account, published in an Irish magazine.

A popular Irish magazine, *The Catholic Bulletin*, published an extraordinary story concerning the Little Flower. The article, reprinted in *The Western People*, was based on a conversation between the man who wrote it and a doctor serving at a Red Cross hospital in France. The hospital, which was situated not far from the French frontlines, was run by an order of nuns.

The doctor was most impressed by the skill of the nuns, especially with the work they were performing for soldiers wounded in battle. He was particularly taken by their medical knowhow and concern for patients. There was nothing they would not willingly do; no job was too much, no sacrifice too demanding.

On one occasion, following a particularly violent battle, the doctor travelled with a convoy of ambulances to collect wounded soldiers and bring back the dead. The battlefield was a scene of carnage. Having filled the ambulances, he decided to stay on the front line, care for the wounded who remained there, and await the return of his colleagues.

He noticed one soldier who appeared to be alive but, on closer inspection, turned out to be dead. There was something notable about his demeanour, which caught the doctor's eye. Not only did the soldier seem at peace but it was almost as if he had been smiling before he died. Stranger still, there was a tiny, fresh white flower in his hand. The doctor was puzzled by how it got there.

Moving on, he encountered another soldier with the same look of calmness and tranquillity on his face. Once again, he clutched a little flower in his lifeless hand. The next soldier was exactly the same – peaceful and at ease, his fingers embracing a fresh flower. "How could this be happening?" the doctor wondered. "What could be going on?"

Glancing up at the battlefield in search of an explanation, he suddenly realised that he had company. Not far ahead of him was a nun, clutching a bunch of white flowers in her hand. She was kneeling beside a soldier, whispering gently to him while placing a little flower in his lifeless hand.

Realising that he was there, she stood up and turned to face him. He was instantly impressed by her kind, gentle beauty; her sweet face and soft features. Surprised that she was on the battlefield on her own – contrary to her order's rules – and aware that the hour was late, he asked her why she was there.

The nun softly replied that she was caring for her fellow countrymen and attending to the dying. She then bowed to the doctor and quietly moved away, continuing with her acts of kindness, caressing lifeless soldiers with soothing words and placing white flowers in their cold, unmoving hands.

Mystified by what he had witnessed, and worried about the nun being alone, he decided to return to the hospital and ask the reverend mother if everything was in order and who the nun might be. Once the ambulances returned, he first told the stretcher-bearers to leave the nun alone; then he hastily headed back to base.

On arrival, he walked to the nearby convent and rang the bell. The door was answered by one of the sisters, who invited him in. Ushered into a waiting room, he asked to speak to the reverend mother, who soon arrived. They knew each other well.

The doctor recounted his story to the nun, explaining that he had come across one of her sisters on the battlefield. He said she was caring for the dead and dying, whispering to them while placing tiny flowers in their hands. "Which of your nuns might it be?" he wondered.

The reverend mother was surprised and asked if the doctor had caught the nun's name. He explained that he hadn't but that her face was memorable – soft and kind. She, too, was puzzled how one of her congregation had been on the battlefield, especially without permission and at such a late hour. Perhaps it was best, she suggested, that he accompany her to a nearby room and they could ask the other nuns.

On entering the room, the doctor saw the nuns at work, making bandages for the wounded. They were seated around a large table. It wasn't the sisters who caught his eye, however. Instead, his gaze was drawn to a large picture hanging above the fireplace. It contained an unmistakable image of the nun he had met on the battlefield just a short time before.

"That's the nun!" he exclaimed, pointing his finger at the picture. Startled by his tone of voice, all the nuns turned as one towards the wall. On it hung an image of the Little Flower.

Prayer cards and medals depicting Thérèse of Lisieux were exchanged by opposing soldiers during the Christmas Truce of 1914.

One of the most moving events in the history of World War I was witnessed on 25 December 1914. Opposing soldiers laid down their arms, walked from their trenches and met in no man's land. They exchanged Christmas greetings, shared memories, laughed together, and showed each other treasured photographs. They even played a football match, which the Germans won 3 – 2.

The soldiers had little to offer to those they met that day. All they had by way of gifts were cigarettes, military buttons and badges. Some carried with them presents of food, particularly plum puddings. Germans brought over Christmas trees, which had been sent from the homeland to the front.

The soldiers also exchanged prayer cards and medals of St. Thérèse. They were highly-valued possessions, sometimes kept in wallets or uniform pockets; other times, in the case of medals, affixed to their helmets. Many had been provided by mothers, sweethearts or wives. That Christmas morning, the Sisters of Mercy had distributed further supplies of relics to the troops.

The soldiers produced these precious religious souvenirs and swapped them with their bitter foes. They were slow to do so, believing they had protected them in battle. "They were very loth to give any souvenirs off these helmets," one soldier wrote in a letter home. "Unless you had any to give in exchange you got none."

That remarkable outbreak of compassion and kindness, so often linked to Christmas, had broken out spontaneously on Christmas Eve 1914. Despite an appeal by Pope Benedict XV for a temporary ceasefire, the warring countries had turned it down. To the contrary, the lead-up to the festive season brought many scenes of devastation.

"The air is split with screeching shells going in various directions," one Irish soldier remarked in *The Ulster Herald.*

Clouds of yellow smoke, showers of earth, flying fragments of iron, snipers' bullets and the "rat-rat-rat" of machineguns filled the air. "Picture the same scene at night – star shells going up in all directions, lighting up the battlefield....One gets lost almost with the ceaseless activity. It is indescribable."

All that changed as darkness settled in on Christmas Eve. "It was a hard, cold and clear night," a Cork soldier, J. F. Hayes, described in a letter to his family. "About 7.30 pm the German lines were lit up by numerous lights, which turned out to be scores of candles on Christmas trees, and all burning brightly. Following the appearance of the lights the Germans began singing as loud as they could....We listened for a moment, not a shot was fired by either side and even not for many hours afterwards."

The precise sequence of events that followed varied from one sector to another along the 440-mile-long Western Front. "They sang *Silent Night – Stille Nacht*. I shall never forget it, it was one of the highlights of my life," one soldier recalled. Another recollected: "First the Germans would sing one of their carols and then we would sing one of ours, until when we started up *O Come, All Ye Faithful* the Germans immediately joined in singing the same hymn to the Latin words *Adeste Fideles*."

Midnight Masses were celebrated by both sides. Some were held by soldier-priests in the trenches, where the troops joined in the singing. Even non-believers participated. One officer remarked on the "painful contrast between the sacred words breathing of 'peace and goodwill' and the deadly struggle upon which the singers are engaged."

Other Masses were held at nearby ruined buildings. "A soldier-priest, having procured an altar-stone, wine, and vestments, an altar was hastily erected against the wall of a farmhouse, half destroyed by the shells," a war correspondent wrote. "It consisted of a door laid upon two high stools." The silence at the service was "impressive beyond words." The soldier-priest would "never forget the midnight Mass of Christmas 1914," an officer said. "Neither shall I!" he added.

The strange peaceful calm carried over to the following morning. "I remember the silence, the eerie sound of silence," a soldier reflected. "All I'd heard for two months in the trenches was the hissing, cracking and whining of bullets in flight, machinegun fire and distant German voices. But there was a dead silence that morning, right across the land as far as you could see."

The silence was soon broken, but not by the sound of cannon or mortar; instead, through the silence came the sound of human voices. "A couple of hours after daybreak, one of the Germans shouted across four times: 'A happy Christmas, English,'" recalled the Cork soldier we heard from earlier. "I did not hear any of our chaps returning the compliment. I guessed that was why he shouted four times.

"About 11.30 am I heard a commotion going on in the next trench, and heard somebody say 'Germans.' I looked up over the parapet of the trench towards the German lines, and lo and behold there were eight or nine Germans advancing from their trenches without arms. The order was quickly passed down 'nobody to fire.'

"They came about half-way, and then halted and shouted and waved hands and a handkerchief. One of ours got up over the trenches, whilst an Irishman followed suit, and they went forward and shook hands with the Germans. Within a few minutes the Germans and English alike were out between the lines in dozens and shaking hands and talking to each other. To look upon the scene you would be under the impression that the war had just ended."

Unfortunately, the conflict was far from over. For most, it resumed again within 24 hours and that warm, affectionate time when bitter enemies embraced would be just a memory. The event, which was frowned upon by commanders, would never happen again. Instead, as the Cork soldier explained, the opposing sides resumed the exchange of souvenirs, but this time they weren't prayer cards or medals of Thérèse; rather, they were "deadly." By deadly, he meant "bullets."

Holy medals and other mementoes of Thérèse of Lisieux were credited with the miraculous survival of soldiers from the "Yankee Division" during a major battle. Many of these soldiers were Irish-Americans.

Irish-American servicemen from New England formed the backbone of the 26th Infantry Division of the United States Army fighting in World War I. They were known as the "Yankee Division", with their nickname chosen to reflect the area of the country – the "Yankee" north-east – they came from. The division found itself in the thick of the action in France after they were posted there in 1917.

The "Yankee Division" – with the letters "YD" inscribed on their insignia – had Rev. George Connor as one of its chaplains and Major James H. McDade as a senior officer. Both were of Irish-American stock, with Connor hailing from Holyoke, Massachusetts, and McDade coming from Boston in the same state. Not only was Boston regarded as Ireland's second capital, but Holyoke – with Irish immigrants drawn to its paper and textile mills – was often referred to as "Ireland Parish".

It happened on one occasion that another chaplain in the division – not Rev. Connor – was wounded and instructed to temporarily withdraw from day-to-day action. During his time off, he decided to visit the Carmel in Lisieux. While there, he spoke with the nuns and, before heading back to the front, was given a collection of medals and mementoes featuring the Little Flower. These he intended to distribute among the troops.

Not long after his return, the division was summoned into action and ordered to advance on the heavily-fortified area around Metz, in north-east France. There the Germans lay in wait, protected by an impregnable array of defences. By any standards, the mission was fraught with danger, and casualties were likely to be high.

On the evening preceding the attack, the chaplain gathered the troops together and delivered an address. "Tomorrow," he said, "we are making a move. I want each of you boys, Catholic, Protestant and Jew, to put one of these souvenirs of the Little Flower in a pocket of your shirt. Although tomorrow will be a perilous movement, not one of you boys will be killed."

His remarks worried Major McDade who, although a Catholic, feared what the comment might do to his troops. Speaking to Rev. George Connor, he said: "Do you know, Father, I was terribly upset when I heard the chaplain say what he did to the boys. I knew well what a perilous task lay before us, and I thought the result of the action would be to shake the faith of our Catholic boys. However, I could not dwell on the matter long, as I had to assemble our captains and prepare the ground for the forthcoming attack."

At 5 am, the soldiers of the "Yankee Division" scaled their trenches – "went over the top" – and advanced on the German line. Like most attacks in World War I, the procedure was semi-suicidal. The only hope was that a sufficiently large number of waves of unfortunate men would overwhelm the enemy, and success would be achieved. Only at the end of the battle would divisional command be able to assess the damage.

After the battle's conclusion, Major McDade spoke again to Rev. George Connor. The news was startling. "On reassembling the battalion after the action," he remarked, "and getting the various company commanders' reports, the extraordinary fact was revealed that not only had none of our men been killed, but not one in the entire battalion was even wounded."

This outcome – as anyone familiar with the battles of World War I would be aware – was hard to believe. The word "miracle" was soon being mentioned, with Connor and McDade believing that that is exactly what it was. Not only had Catholics survived but Protestants and Jews had survived, too, prompting both men to believe that the "Providence of God covers all."

Dublin-born priest, Fr. Willie Doyle, became one of the great Irish heroes of World War I. An early devotee of the Little Flower, he died at the infamous Third Battle of Ypres in 1917.

The year 1912 was a memorable one in Irish history, although not always for the best of reasons. Home Rule dominated the headlines, with huge rallies in Dublin supporting self-government and equally enormous demonstrations opposing it in Belfast. In April, the *Titanic* sank. James Joyce left Ireland for the last time. Even British Prime Minister Asquith, who was the target of an arson and hatchet attack on his visit to Dublin, must have been happy to leave the country.

In November 1912, a priest by the name of Fr. Willie Doyle also left Ireland, intending to visit the holy sites of France. Aged 39, he had been ordained to the priesthood only five years earlier. Born into a privileged family in Dalkey, County Dublin, this highly-intelligent Jesuit had, since his ordination, been holding missions and retreats around Ireland. Although excellent at his work – his missions were described as electrifying – he was restless and in search of something new. He found it during his visit to France.

"When leaving Ireland I did not think my journey was to mean so much for myself spiritually," Fr. Doyle later recalled. "At Lourdes, at Tours, at Angers, and other places, our dearest Lord seemed to have had His message prepared and waiting for me." Visiting Lisieux, however, had the greatest impact: "I had a feeling all along that my visit to Lisieux would do much for me, and I was not mistaken; so that I am coming home like a bee laden with the honey of God, which I pray Him not to allow me to squander or misuse."

The "honey" he brought home was the simple philosophy of Thérèse – her little way. He was smitten by the idea that what matters is the mundane and seemingly unimportant, not the performance of great and mighty deeds. The profundity of her uncomplicated insight struck him in an instant. No longer was sanctity the domain of those with the strength to endure great austerity. No longer would small, daily sacrifices be subservient to heroic deeds. From then on, everything mattered; everyone, in their daily lives, could be a saint.

"Kneeling at the grave of the Little Flower, I gave myself into her hands to guide and to make me a saint," he remarked. "I promised her to make it the rule of my whole life, every day without exception, to seek in all things my greater mortification, to give all and to refuse nothing. I have made this resolution with great confidence because I realise how utterly it is beyond my strength; but I feel the Little Flower will get me grace to keep it perfectly."

It didn't take long for Fr. Doyle to discover the perfect setting to implement Thérèse's little way – the battlefields of World War I. In November 1914 – exactly two years after his visit to Lisieux – he volunteered as a military chaplain and was duly appointed to the 8th Royal Irish Fusiliers, 16th Division. He eventually participated in some of the greatest battles of the war, at Ginchy, Guillemont and at the Somme.

On the battlefields, Fr. Doyle prayed with and cared for the men. He offered solace to the injured and said prayers for the dead. He loved his men – his "boys" he called them – and seldom left their side. Showing extraordinary bravery, he would crawl to a moaning soldier in no man's land, offer succour to a half-mangled body in a trench, or soothe the shattered nerves of someone who was shellshocked. He never cared which religion the men belonged to. "Ah, Father," one wounded Ulsterman said to him, "I don't belong to your Church." "No," said Fr. Doyle, "but you belong to my God."

He also said Mass for the combatants in the most horrific conditions. "By cutting a piece out of the side of the trench I was just able to stand in front of my tiny altar, a biscuit box supported on two German bayonets," he wrote in a letter after the Battle of the Somme. "God's angels, no doubt, were hovering overhead, but so were the shells, hundreds of them, and I was a little afraid that when the earth shook with the crash of the guns, the chalice might be overturned.

"Round about me on every side was the biggest congregation I ever had; behind the altar, on either side, and in front, row after row, sometimes crowding one upon the other, but all quiet and silent, as if they were straining their ears to catch every syllable of that tremendous act of Sacrifice – but every man was dead!" Some had lain there for a week; others had just fallen, "but there they lay, for none had time to bury them, brave fellows, every one, friend and foe alike."

In December 1916, Fr. Doyle was transferred to the 8th Battalion of the Royal Dublin Fusiliers. The battalion ended up fighting in the Third Battle of Ypres, in August 1917. That same month, in mid-August, he wrote what was to prove to be his final letter to his father. A few days later, he was dead.

As with many events of war, it is unclear how he died. It seems that he was attending to a soldier who lay wounded in an exposed position, having crawled to him under enemy fire.

We don't know whether his presence attracted further attention, but we do know that the bombardment became vicious. As the *Irish Weekly* noted: "Then came a screeching shell, a mighty rumble of raging earth, and when the smoke had cleared away brave Fr. Willie had drained the martyr's cup – beside his 'own brave boys'."

The story of Fr. Doyle's tragic death, aged 44, made headline news back home. His courage in the face of danger was highlighted. His saintly qualities were noted. It wasn't long before people were revering him – and praying to him – as if he were a saint. It didn't take long, either, before demands surfaced for his beatification. Clearly, the public loved him, including the author Brendan Behan who, in later years, referred to him in *Borstal Boy*.

Not long after his death, notices began to appear in newspaper personal columns thanking him for favours received. Fittingly, one of those notices contained the following: "Most heartfelt thanksgiving to St.Thérèse, Little Flower of Jesus, and to Fr. William Doyle, for many temporal favours received through their intercession." Whoever wrote the note was probably unaware of the link between the two individuals in question.

But there was no escaping the connection. Throughout the war, Fr. Doyle's actions had reflected the thinking of the Little Flower. Everything mattered. Nothing was too small. Each act of kindness and compassion was important. All things were done for the love of God. And it all dated back to that day in November 1912 when he was overcome, as he put it, by a sense of "peace and strength" while praying at the grave of the Little Flower.

An Irish soldier's miraculous cure, attributed to Thérèse of Lisieux, hit the headlines in August 1917.

An extraordinary recovery from hearing and speech loss resulting from shellshock was reported by Laois man and British Army recruit, Private Stephen Conroy, towards the end of August 1917. A member of the Leinster Regiment, he had been rendered deaf and without speech at Armentières, northern France, just short of the Franco-Belgian border, which was the scene of heavy fighting during World War I.

After spending many weeks in a French hospital, he was removed to England and eventually transferred to the King George V Hospital in Dublin, where he languished for six months showing no signs of recovery. All that changed in mid-August 1917 when he was removed to Jervis Street Hospital, where he was given the Little Flower's book to read.

The book was presented to him by the sister in charge of his ward. She also suggested that he should make a novena to the future saint. This he did, praying fervently despite the fact that, although he was aware of the Sacred Heart, he had never heard of the Little Flower.

On Saturday, 25 August, Private Conroy was overcome by a feeling that his affliction would disappear the following day. He mentioned this in a note to a member of the hospital staff. He awoke between two o'clock and three o'clock the next morning, feeling thirsty. Because the night nurse was at the other end of the ward, he was unable to call for a drink. She then exited the room, following which he turned over on his elbow to await her return. Instantly, something extraordinary occurred.

"I saw a lady standing over my bed," he later explained. "She was the same as the picture of the Little Flower on the day of her First Communion." He added that it was a "white form, all dazzling light" with "a wreath of flowers on her head, stooping over the bed to me, and she said something to me, which I can't remember. Then she said, 'Say three Hail Marys morning and evening.'" He also noted that the figure moved to a nearby table on which stood a crucifix. She stood there, looking at him for a minute or so, before walking out the door.

A short time later, the nurse returned to the ward and the soldier, on impulse, shouted, "Nurse, nurse." As one newspaper reported: "The poor nurse fell back with fright against the wall, and, as she herself said, she felt she was 'stuck to the wall' when she heard this man, deaf and dumb for six months, crying out to her in the silence of the ward. She went over to him and gave him a drink, and found not only could he speak but could hear everything she said to him."

The newspaper then continued: "The poor soldier was very excited, and beads of perspiration showed on his forehead. He told her all he had seen. 'The vision,' he said, 'was like one of the pictures in the Little Flower book.' 'Which one was it?' asked the nurse. There were several pictures of her in the book, taken at different periods of her life. 'This one,' he said, opening the book and pointing to the picture of the Little Flower as a first communicant, with wreath and veil, 'only,' said he, 'she was all dazzling light.'"

Although it is tempting to dismiss Conroy's miracle as having a more conventional explanation, this point of view was not shared by medical experts. As the Jervis Street throat and ear specialist, P. J. Keogh, who treated Conroy, explained, the case was a remarkable one which "had been looked upon very unfavourably from a medical point of view." He noted that the condition had persisted for a long time – well over six months – that the victim was 54 years old, and that cures in cases of this kind were few and far between.

The consultant added that the prognosis had been "distinctly bad," especially considering that the seats of speech and hearing in the brain are so far apart and that no precedents could be recalled where both were restored at one and the same moment. The specialist ended his remarks by saying that when the cure was reported to the King George V Hospital, the authorities there were astonished that Conroy "should have recovered at all."

Fr. Myles Ronan, one of the hospital chaplains who had attended Conroy, also noted, as the *Evening Herald* reported, that "Conroy was in his normal senses the night prior to the cure, and there is certainly nothing in the man's demeanour to suggest the slightest inaccuracy in the marvellous story he has related." Conroy, he said, was "wide awake, and there was nothing remarkable to account for any terrible excitant of the nervous system. He can speak and hear now as well as ever he did, and he only began to speak and hear after he saw the vision."

In the following weeks, the story of Private Stephen Conroy dominated news coverage in the press, featuring not only in national publications but in local papers including *The Cork Examiner, The Skibbereen Eagle, The Munster Express, Nenagh News, The Drogheda Independent* and *The Anglo-Celt*, among others. Significantly, the soldier retained his ability to speak and hear, with the *Evening Herald* noting that he continued to converse "freely and joyously with those who were permitted to see him." More importantly, the paper pointed out that he was "unshaken in his belief that his cure was due to the intercession of the Little Flower."

Within a month of the previous miracle, another extraordinary recovery was reported in Dublin.

Four weeks after Private Conroy regained his speech and hearing, a similar revival occurred in Dublin. This time the cure involved a 28-year-old Derry soldier, who was confined with the after-effects of shellshock in Dublin's King George V Hospital. A private in the Royal Irish Regiment, Francis Donaghy had been seriously injured in one of the most renowned battles of the Great War.

Donaghy had fought in the Battle of Messines, which took place in Flanders, on the Western Front, in June 1917. It was a vicious engagement, involving heavy artillery bombardments and ground combat. Some 10,000 German soldiers were killed in one series of explosions alone. The noise was so loud that it could be heard in Dublin and by Lloyd George in his Downing Street study. Tens of thousands of soldiers were killed; others ended up traumatised and suffering from shellshock.

Donaghy emerged from the battle without speech or hearing. A shell had fallen on top of the trench where he was stationed, tumbling the trench in. On recovering consciousness, he found he was unable to speak or hear. Although treated at various hospitals in England, he showed no signs of improvement. During the summer of 1917, he was transferred to Dublin, where doctors concluded he was incurable. He decided to place his fate in the hands of Thérèse of Lisieux.

During his stay in the King George V Hospital, Donaghy befriended another patient, a Donegal man by the name of William Joseph McDonagh, who was a former member of the Irish Guards. One evening, the two men were allowed a brief respite from the hospital and went in search of a church. They ended up at the Church of St. Francis Xavier, Gardiner Street, where a retreat was being held by the Jesuit priest, Rev. Thomas Murphy.

Around eight o'clock, just at the recitation of the third mystery of the rosary, his companion noticed that Private Donaghy was becoming restless and excited. Suddenly, Donaghy said, in quick breaths, "I can speak," and almost immediately murmured, "I can hear." The companion, in a later interview, remarked that he was "very startled" by what had happened. He became even more alarmed when Donaghy showed signs of collapse.

Members of the congregation, who were attracted to the commotion, helped Donaghy out of the church. On reaching the corridor, it appeared that his condition was very serious. He was shivering and on the verge of delirium. After a period of unconsciousness, he asked, "Where am I?" Showing no improvement, and fearing he was about to die, those attending him summoned a priest.

Soon, Donaghy was well enough to be brought outside. There he suffered a relapse. Although his hands and frame trembled violently, he was well enough to say that he felt "supremely happy." An ambulance was summoned and he was transported back to hospital. Before departing, he was still trembling, excited and weak. On arrival, he had improved greatly. His speech, which had initially seemed inarticulate, eventually returned to its natural state.

The following day, Donaghy's recovery became front-page news. The *Evening Herald*'s headline read "Sensational: Cure of Deaf and Dumb Soldier." A day later, *The Freeman's Journal* trumpeted "Cure in City Church: The Remarkable Case of Private Donaghy." *The Derry People and Donegal News* – Donaghy's local paper – proclaimed "Miraculous Cure: Hearing and Speech Recovered."

The *Evening Telegraph* – Ireland's leading evening newspaper at the time – visited the hospital and interviewed the patient in his bed. Although still in a nervous state, they reported that "both his hearing and speech seemed perfect." He explained that prior to his recovery he had been making a novena to the Little Flower, which concluded on the previous Thursday. It was at the end of the novena that he and his friend had entered the church in Gardiner Street to say a few prayers.

"A flash of light came across my eyes," he told the newspaper reporter. "I felt a kind of choking at my heart. I reached up my two hands as the light was passing." Asked if it might have been the ordinary chapel lights, he responded: "No. It was not the ordinary light at all. It was a very, very silvery light. It made no heat or anything. It came gently past. It came from the left-hand side where I was kneeling. I reached out my hand to grasp the seat, and called my comrade....I fainted then."

The *Evening Telegraph* made further inquiries to the hospital and were told that the patient was improving and was "able to speak and hear quite well." It was confirmed that his cure had "excited a good deal of interest at the hospital," where his case had been regarded as practically hopeless.

As for Donaghy's view on the matter, he remarked that, although he was still weak from excitement, his joy was unbounded. "You can hardly understand what it means to be able to speak," he said. He added that it was no coincidence that he had been praying to Thérèse for some time. "This," he concluded, "is another cure for the Little Flower."

SOARING ON
EAGLES WINGS

Thérèse would have enjoyed the decades between the two world wars. For a cloistered nun, in the nineteenth century, she was astonishingly forward-looking. The growing popularity of the gramophone, radio and telephone would have appealed to her. She would have also been intrigued by the increasing power of cinema.

Thérèse loved new technology. Even when confined in the Carmel at Lisieux, she was transfixed by the use of the elevator or lift. She marvelled at its ability to bring people, at speed, from one level to another. Just like the lift, she thought, her little way would transport people quickly to God.

As it turned out, the new technologies helped to spread Thérèse's thinking and consolidate her fame. News agencies instantly reported her beatification and canonisation to the world. Radio broadcasts brought her into people's homes. Films told the story of her life. Famous celebrities, cardinals and converts to Catholicism propagated her name.

One of Ireland's favourite singing stars from the 1930s – 1960s, the French singer Édith Piaf, developed a lifelong devotion to St. Thérèse following receipt of a miraculous cure in the early 1920s.

During the golden age of radio, few voices appealed to Irish audiences more than the sweet voice of Édith Piaf. The timing of the French chanteuse's life was perfect. Born just before Christmas 1915, her first recording was released in 1936, not long after Radio Éireann had switched to its high-powered transmitter beaming nationwide from Athlone. By the 1950s and early 1960s, when almost every Irish home possessed a Pye, Bush, Marconi, Philips or Murphy radio set, her songs *La Vie en Rose* and *Non, Je Ne Regrette Rien* were international blockbuster hits.

Early Radio Éireann schedules reflected the popularity of this acclaimed Parisian star. Her songs were featured on all the main music programmes of the time, as well as on special broadcasts dedicated to her extraordinary life and career. Among the latter were a Radio Éireann broadcast in 1954 featuring special recordings made by Radiodiffusion-Télévision Française, and a 1960 radio programme, *Music for Moderns*, containing an "outstanding contribution" from Piaf, as noted by a reviewer in the *Irish Independent*.

Known as The Little Sparrow because of her diminutive height (4ft 8in), on the surface Piaf shared little in common with St. Thérèse apart from the closeness of her nickname to the saint's Little Flower. Abandoned by her mother at birth, she was brought up for a time at her grandmother's brothel in Normandy, where she was cared for by prostitutes. She eventually took to the streets, where she scraped a living as a singer, became an unmarried mother and had a succession of affairs including, later on, a passionate but ultimately broken relationship with the film star Yves Montand.

Her only child died aged two from meningitis. To make matters worse, the love of her life, boxer Marcel Cerdan, was killed in an air crash in 1949 while on his way to meet her in

New York. Married twice, she ended up with severe addictions to morphine and alcohol, which were exacerbated by a series of car accidents. Not surprisingly, she died young, aged 47, from liver cancer. It would be hard to imagine a life with a trajectory more dissimilar to the simple path taken by the Little Flower.

Contrary to what we might expect, however, there was no one more devoted to St. Thérèse than Édith Piaf. The reason was simple – she believed that Thérèse had been responsible for curing a serious eye condition she had as a child. Known as keratitis, it presents as a painful inflammation of the cornea and is often caused by infection involving bacteria, viruses, fungi or parasites. It can result in blurred vision and sight loss. In Édith's case, the condition was progressing steadily and she was gradually becoming blind.

Despite repeated praying by the brothel's occupants on the child's behalf, no cure was forthcoming. Entreaties to Thérèse, who had died not much more than two decades earlier, were producing no results. Things were looking serious. As Édith put it, she crashed into everything and had to walk with her hands extended in front. With her sense of sight disappearing, she lived in a world of sounds and words.

Aware that a four-year-old child named Reine Fouquet had recovered from a similar condition having prayed at Thérèse's grave, the decision was taken at the brothel to travel to Lisieux. "If Thérèse cured that little girl, she will cure my Édith," the grandmother said as she, along with other occupants of the household, departed on their journey.

Although Thérèse had yet to be canonised, thousands of pilgrims were already flocking to her resting place, seeking cures for their illnesses and solace from the many afflictions pervading their lives. The new arrivals, including Édith, joined the supplicants and prayed to Thérèse. Before they departed, they scooped up clay from the future saint's grave. It is said that, in the following days, they applied the clay to Édith's eyes.

Little more than a week later, Édith declared that she could see. Her sight had recovered, the keratitis was gone, her childhood restored. Piaf never doubted that she had received a miraculous cure. From then on, she always wore a medal around her neck commemorating Thérèse and, in later life, kept a statue of the saint beside her bed and on the table in her many stage dressing rooms. She adopted Thérèse as her patron saint, praying to her and seeking her protection, while always thanking the saint for bringing her one of the happiest days of her life – "The day I regained my eyesight."

Although Piaf lived for another 40 years, there weren't too many other happy days to remember. True, she went on to become an international star, achieving worldwide acclaim as a singer, songwriter and actress. True, also, her voice became known as one of the strongest, most passionate and most quintessentially French of all time. But her life was indelibly blighted by tragedy and there was always an overshadowing sadness reflected in her songs, which were so full of sorrow, love and loss.

Given the affection of the Irish for Édith Piaf, it was no surprise that her decline into ill-health in 1963 was covered extensively in the national media. Newspapers speculated on the nature of her illness, her hoped-for recovery, and the subsequent reports that the end was near. Her death from cancer, on 10 October 1963, aged 47, was front-page news. So, also, was her interment at Père Lachaise cemetery, where the Archbishop of Paris refused her a Church burial on account of her immoral lifestyle.

Everyone else seemed to forgive her. *The Irish Press* reported that "more than 40,000" people lined the roads of Paris as her body passed by; another 15,000 thronged the cemetery. Mourners "crashed through steel barriers" to say their goodbyes, the *Evening Herald* added. Thousands had already queued outside her apartment to pay their last respects, according to *The Cork Examiner*, adding that those who were admitted witnessed her body in the library, next to the singer's open piano.

How many mourners ventured into the singer's bedroom is not recorded by the national press. Had they done so, they would have noticed the small picture of St. Thérèse on Édith's bedside table. It had never left her side, right up to her death, acting as a reminder of the great benefactor who watched over her in illness and health, and brought her the cure from failing eyesight that had changed her life as a child.

The beatification of Thérèse, in April 1923, marked a hugely important step on her road to sainthood. It created quite a stir in Ireland.

Irish people prayed for the beatification of Thérèse shortly after she rose to prominence in the national press. Prayers and novenas were called for in the hope of furthering her cause. Details of miracles and cures were requested to be sent to the relevant authorities assessing her case. A special Christmas novena was held to ensure her beatification might be "speedy."

"All the clients of the Little Flower, so many of whom are to be found in Ireland, will redouble their prayers that soon she may be raised to the altars of the Church," one newspaper columnist remarked. Another asked that all those who received favours from her should send them to named Church authorities in Dublin. "Any communication thus received will also be dispatched to Lisieux, in order to further, if necessary, the cause of her beatification," it was advised.

We might ask, why the sudden interest in beatifying the Little Flower? "In this materialistic age it is soul-refreshing to come across a life like that of the nun of Lisieux," one commentator, writing in early 1913, remarked. "It forces one to remember that the Catholic Church is just as potent for producing sanctity in this age of airships as it was in Bridget's time, when minstrels sang of the glories of Erin....Little Thérèse of the Infant Jesus and the Holy Face is but another proof of that."

Even if some of the rhetoric was occasionally overblown, it seems to have hit the mark. By early 1923, all was set for the beatification event in Rome. Thérèse had already been declared venerable in 1921; beatification was the next step on the road to canonisation or sainthood, which would take a little while longer.

Two miracles, attributed to Thérèse, had already been app-roved. One involved a cure from chronic stomach ulcers. It was said that, in 1916, Thérèse had appeared to the sufferer and promised she would get better soon. The following morning, rose petals were found strewn around her bed. A few days later, she fully recovered – her cure being confirmed by X-rays and reports from reputable doctors.

The second miracle involved a young man who was dying from tuberculosis. He, too, prayed to Thérèse, having pressed one of her relics to his heart. An immediate restoration to health was reported. "The destroyed and ravaged lungs have been replaced by new lungs, carrying out their normal functions and about to revive the entire organism," the man's doctor reported. "A slight emaciation persists, which will disappear within a few days under a regularly assimilated diet."

The formal, and colourful, beatification ceremonies were held in Rome on Sunday, 29 April 1923. St. Peter's Basilica was awash with colour. Columns were draped with gold-fringed crimson brocade hangings. Thousands of sparkling lights shone on the rich robes of the cardinals. An illuminated picture of Thérèse was on prominent display. "The ceremonies were marked by a return to the splendour which formerly characterised these celebrations. Nothing was wanting of colour, light and beauty to impress the spectator," one wire service report commented.

Crowds arrived at St. Peter's from five o'clock in the morning, anxious to secure the best vantage points for the ceremony scheduled to begin at 9.30 am. The solemn proceedings started on time. A Vatican archivist read the formal Brief, in which the virtues of Thérèse were extolled. The Brief was then shown to the congregation. Next, her relics were exposed, along with two enormous panels of the Little Flower, one inside and the other outside the basilica.

Instantly, the bells of St. Peter's rang out in a crescendo of sound. It was like "a peal of joy," one newsman remarked. This was followed by the Bishop of Bayeux intoning the *Te Deum* and incensing the relics and pictures of Thérèse. After High Mass and special prayers, the ceremony was brought to a close.

That afternoon, at 5.30, a second ceremony, involving the pope, took place. Again, it was a magnificent event, involving a colourful papal procession, benediction and the choir of the Julian Chapel. Among the offerings were a silk portrait of Thérèse, a bound narrative of her life, and a reliquary containing fragments of her bones. At the close, the procession traversed the length of the basilica between two lines of Palatine Guards. As the pope departed, the famous silver bugles sounded the *Triumphal March*.

Back in Ireland, there was widespread elation. A Mass of thanksgiving was offered in Meath Street, Dublin, while a lecture to commemorate "The Little Flower Beatification" was held at Dublin city's Mansion House. This latter venue was "crowded," newspapers reported, with the speaker, Rev. M. MacMahon, saying that what had taken place in Rome was destined "to exercise a direct and immediate influence on the spiritual life of today."

And so it was, on 29 April 1923, that the beatification ceremonies came to an end and another step was taken on the road to the canonisation of the Little Flower. Reflecting on the event that day, one commentator remarked that, without doubt, Thérèse's "humility was her greatness; her littleness was her power." Now that she was beatified, he concluded, her power would be even more pronounced – bringing "confidence to the timid," inspiring hope in the weak, and inflaming the tepid with "love that dares all for God."

The recitation of novenas to St. Thérèse grew rapidly in Ireland following her beatification.

The practice of reciting novenas finds its roots in very early Christianity and in pre-Christian Greece and Rome. The word "novena" – from the Latin "novem", meaning nine – gives us a clue to its origin. In classical Greece and Rome, families mourned their dead for nine days. Early Christians also attributed significance to the number nine, pointing out, among other matters, how Jesus gave up his spirit on the cross at the ninth hour.

In time, Christians began practising the recitation of prayers for nine consecutive days, often leading up to the feast of a chosen saint, and usually to seek a special favour or grace. By the time of Thérèse, they were commonly recited in the Carmel. As a young nun, she prepared herself for a difficult and trying retreat by saying a novena. When she was dying, her fellow sisters recited one to Our Lady of Victories seeking a miracle, but to no avail.

After her death, the roles were reversed and novenas were recited to Thérèse. They became popular in Ireland in the 1920s. One newspaper advertisement, in *The Meath Chronicle*, notified readers of a forthcoming special novena in honour of Thérèse, to be held in Dunlavin. It began on a Tuesday and ended nine days later, on her feast day. Another one – this time in Limerick – was advertised in the *Limerick Leader* and, once again, ended nine days later, on her feast day.

The latter event had seen "crowded congregations" in attendance, the *Limerick Leader* commented. A further novena to Thérèse, in the same city – this time at St. Joseph's Church – was said to "have become very popular with the faithful, who attend in large numbers from every part of the city." The church had installed a statue of the Little Flower which, the newspaper reported, was "decorated with a profusion of flowers and lighted with multicoloured electric bulbs" in honour of the novena.

Interest was stirred by positive reports in the press of favours received and miracles occurring, all thanks to Thérèse, and all following novenas. As far back as 1917, *The Liberator*, which was published out of Tralee, carried a thanksgiving note for a cure. "A cure of a very miraculous nature has taken place after novenas to St. Thérèse of the Child Jesus and Our Blessed Lady of Mercy, which is vouched for by the doctor, sisters and nurses, and for which the undersigned begs to offer grateful thanks."

Other reports of cures came from abroad. In 1927, *The Kerry News* advised readers of an Irish-American woman's cure in New Bedford, Massachusetts. The woman – Miss Alice M. Toomey – had, for more than eight years, suffered from a foot crushed by mill machinery. In 1925, she attended a novena to the Little Flower.

"For nine days she attended all the services, and a relic of the saint was applied to her wounded foot," the report informed us. "On the last day, as she knelt before the shrine, she sought to move her foot and found the pain as great as ever, but upon rising she found she could walk comfortably. She relinquished her cane and walked home. Physicians who examined the foot pronounced it normal again."

Another report – this time from Budapest – was chronicled in *The Munster Express*. The story concerned a typist who had just lost her job following a rationalisation programme in the government department she worked for. She was particularly troubled by her situation as she had to support her aged mother. "There seemed no likelihood of her securing another equally remunerative post," the newspaper remarked.

One day, a copy of *Story of a Soul* came her way and, having read it, she resolved to say a novena – or "nine days' appeal," as the newspaper put it – to the saint. The ninth and last visit to the Carmelite church, where the novena was being held, coincided with the day when the typist's employment ended.

Unknown to her, on that day the head of the department in which she worked received an unannounced visit from a young nun. The newspaper continued the story: "On being asked what she desired, the nun said that she had come to plead for the reinstatement of the dismissed typist. The chief declared himself unable to move in the matter; but, when the nun firmly announced her intention of remaining until he decided to grant her request, he was surprised to find himself agreeing to revoke the dismissal.

"The door had scarcely closed on the departing nun when the typist knocked and entered. The chief, nonplussed at his inexplicable capitulation, told her to call back the nun she had sent to plead her cause. But the girl denied all knowledge of the nun, and when the employees in the outer rooms, and the hall porter were questioned, it transpired that no nun had been seen to enter the building.

"A scene of confusion followed, during which the tearful typist, pleading her innocence, drew from her satchel a little book, and saying, 'This is the only nun I know anything about.'" She opened the book and displayed the photograph of St. Thérèse, at the sight of which her boss declared without hesitation, "Yes, that was she!"

The Munster Express concluded: "It is, perhaps, superfluous to add that the typist remains at her post." It went on to state that the occurrence, while vouched for and testified to by reliable witnesses, was accepted as a "miracle" by the religiously-inclined, as a "successful materialisation" by the psychically-minded and as an "optical illusion" by the sceptical.

From the 1920s – 1950s, tens of thousands of novenas to St. Thérèse were held all over Ireland. That era was not just about novenas, but also about confraternities, sodalities, the proliferation of holy cards and meatless Fridays. Although these forms of devotion – especially novenas – have not disappeared, they are much fewer in number than they were in their golden era in the half-century following the death of Thérèse of Lisieux.

A Catholic priest, of Irish lineage, set up a famous Scottish grotto to Our Lady and St. Thérèse in 1922. It became popular with Irish pilgrims in the 1920s and '30s.

The 1920s were tough years for the coal miners of Scotland. The industry had been in decline for years. Output was tumbling, wages falling, and the work, which was tough, was scarce. Mine owners wanted pay cuts and longer hours. The Miners' Federation put its foot down, insisting, "Not a penny off the pay, not a minute on the day." Strikes and shutouts became commonplace.

The mining town of Carfin, in Scotland, was badly hit by the chaos and unrest. Situated close to Motherwell, it had strong Irish links. Its population was mostly Irish and Catholic, its workforce having been imported to work in the mines. Fellow Catholics from Lithuania – pushed out by discrimination and poverty – made up the bulk of the remaining inhabitants.

There was idleness in Carfin in the 1920s. Demoralised workers had little to do. All that changed when a local Catholic priest – Canon Thomas Nimmo Taylor – decided to mobilise the unemployed and build a grotto to Our Lady and Thérèse of Lisieux. This they did in the early 1920s, using whatever spare time they had in the endeavour. The grotto opened on 1 October 1922, with 2,000 people in attendance. It went on to become a "must visit" destination almost overnight.

Canon Taylor, whose mother Rose-Anne came from Irish immigrant stock, was a remarkable man and a great supporter of St. Thérèse. It seems strange now, but their paths almost crossed in real life. As a seminarian in Paris, he regularly undertook adoration at the shrine to the Virgin Mary in the Church of Our Lady of Victories. That was the same church which, a few years earlier, in 1887, was visited by the young Thérèse Martin on her pilgrimage to Rome.

He became one of Thérèse's earliest devotees following her death. Having read *Story of a Soul* in 1901 – shortly after its publication – Canon Taylor was smitten by the simplicity of her way. He immediately began corresponding with the nuns in Lisieux. Four visits followed soon after, during which he spoke, face to face, with those who had recently known the Little Flower. He committed himself to bring her life, virtues and powers of intercession to public attention.

So intense was his devotion that, in 1912, he authored the first popular English translation of her autobiography, which sold in huge numbers. He also testified before the Vatican committee considering Thérèse's cause for canonisation. This he did in Normandy, having just arrived there with a group of

British pilgrims. During his visit, in 1910, the committee was conducting interviews with the nuns, among others.

His grotto in Carfin, after it opened in 1922, went on to enormous success. Pilgrims flocked there from all parts of Britain and Ireland, with tens of thousands arriving each year. Early Irish pilgrims were already arriving by the late 1920s. However, it took until the mid-1930s for organised tours to travel from Ireland – the first from Belfast, and the second from the Irish Free State having been organised by the International Travel Bureau, Dame Street, Dublin.

Interest in the grotto was boosted by stories concerning miracles which, soon after its opening, started to appear in the press. In 1928, a Scottish man, named Stevenson, from Renfrew, with a broken spine and paralysed from the waist down, got up and walked after being blessed with a relic of Thérèse by Canon Taylor. "The doctors who examined Stevenson and Renfrew people who knew his physical state from visitation at his home agree that his restoration to the use of his limbs is a miracle," one newspaper commented.

The following year, a Protestant child who had become paralysed and speechless as a result of meningitis, recovered her faculties after being similarly blessed with a relic. "Immediately there was a marked improvement in her condition," a newspaper noted. "Previously she walked only when someone supported her. Now she walked unaided." On arrival at her home railway station, her father, on seeing his daughter walk, exclaimed, "My God, what has happened?"

Yet another miracle was recorded in 1934, when a victim of rheumatoid arthritis, who was unable to stand and had been confined to bed for over seven years, suddenly exclaimed: "I can walk." Like the other cases before her, she too had been touched with the relic of St. Thérèse. "Her left hand, which had been closed for twelve months, as it was touched with the relic, began to open, and strength came to her feet and legs which enabled her not only to stand up but walk from the grotto into the waiting car," according to the subsequent press account.

With miracles like those being reported, it was no surprise that, from 1922 – 1965, some 10,000 people turned up for the annual Corpus Christi festival at Carfin. At times, that figure soared as high as 50,000. These were remarkable numbers and a tribute to the work of Canon Taylor, who never lost enthusiasm either for his project or for Thérèse.

He also promoted the Little Flower's name abroad, most notably in Ireland which he visited on many occasions. In 1934, he was a visitor to the grotto to Our Lady at Inchicore, Dublin, which had opened in 1930. In addition, he had a brother who was a priest in Ireland and who was later interred at Castleknock.

Taylor's Dublin connections didn't end there. He was a regular visitor to the Carmel in Blackrock, where he became friends with the nuns. Amusingly, he once described how, as early as 1904, he had asked the mother prioress at Blackrock if she thought Thérèse should be canonised. She had laughed and said, "We might as well canonise all the nuns in her monastery." She later changed her mind!

Canon Taylor died in 1963, leaving behind his grotto, which survives to this day. Almost singlehandedly, he was the man who, in Scotland, did most to generate devotion to Thérèse in the early years after her death. "Perfection," he had once written, "could be achieved only by prayer and the constant sublimation of self, with its personal aims and ambitions, to the omnipotent wisdom of the divine plan." Nowhere, he felt, did that assertion come closer to realisation than in the person of Thérèse of Lisieux.

The Irish were present at the ceremony in Rome where Thérèse finally became a saint. The date was 17 May 1925.

A special place was reserved in the Vatican's royal gallery for Timothy Healy, Governor-General of the Irish Free State, who represented Ireland at the canonisation of Thérèse of Lisieux in May 1925. Members of the Corkman's family were located in the nearby papal family gallery, affording them a spectacular view of proceedings.

The 60,000 crowd in the basilica contained many Irish pilgrims, some of them arriving with the 1,100-strong English National Pilgrimage to Rome. Most of the Irish would have been happier if the corresponding 1,000-strong Irish National Pilgrimage had left, as planned, in May. Unfortunately, issues of comfort and cost had led to its postponement until October, when lower temperatures and cheaper fares would prevail.

Nothing could interfere with the splendour of the day. Rome was a sea of grandeur and colour. For some, the highlight was the splendid papal procession, with the pope seated in his ceremonial throne, being carried by 12 red-robed footmen. Behind him was a seemingly endless line of cardinals, archbishops and bishops in their wonderful cassocks and capes. The crowd knelt and cried "Long live the pope" as the entourage passed by. The pope, in turn, gave them his blessing.

The arrival of the pope at St. Peter's was heralded by the famous silver trumpets. He and his entourage entered the basilica.

The interior was bathed in a riot of colour. One hundred thousand candles and electric lights hung from coloured marble pillars. Everything was red, gold or velvet, with the uniforms of the Swiss Guards adding to the glow. Even the guest list was colourful – King Emmanuel of Italy, Queen Amélie of Portugal, representatives of the Bourbon dynasty and of the Braganza, Orléans, Saxon and Austrian royal houses.

"Scores of times a passageway had to be cleared for women and men who had fainted," a commentator observed in *The Cork Examiner*. "Children were clattering all over monuments of the saints for a vantage point, and even women were climbing to the tops of the wooden confessionals....An event strange to the ears and eyes of Anglo-Saxons was the frequent outburst of applause and cheers which greeted Pope Pius."

Even the Mass was of historic proportions, with an "electric loud speaker," as one report called it, bringing the pope's voice to all parts of the basilica for the first time in its history. The use of the newfangled technology – making the pope's voice "audible to all by microphones" – was highlighted in news reports of the canonisation, indicating just how novel the technology was at the time.

The eventual process of canonisation was impressive, too. The pope sat on his throne, while the Cardinal Procurator of Canonisation approached him and prayed for the insertion of Thérèse's name in the list of saints. Following several ceremonial procedures, including the singing of the *Litany of the Saints*, the pope proceeded to the canonisation and intoned the *Te Deum*. He then said a prayer, bringing to an end the wonderful occasion on Sunday, 17 May 1925, when Thérèse of Lisieux – the Little Flower – joined the great pantheon of saints.

There was enormous excitement in Lisieux. For weeks, the townsfolk had been decorating their houses, painting doors and windows, hanging flowers everywhere to commemorate the event. Banners had been erected in the streets. Private ceremonies had been held at the Carmelite convent. Hundreds of townsfolk had travelled to Rome; most stayed behind and congregated in local churches to sing the *Te Deum* at the precise moment the formal canonisation was taking place.

Back in the Eternal City, following the early-morning ceremonies, the long wait commenced for the illumination of the facade and dome of St. Peter's which had been promised for that night. At precisely 8.40 pm, some 680 bitumen flares were lit on the basilica, adding to the light from 5,000 candles in white paper lanterns that lit up the main outline of the structure. Hundreds of thousands of people brought the city to a standstill just to witness the event.

"The enthusiasm of the spectators was only equalled by their amazement," a correspondent reported for the *Irish Independent*. "In the daylight the gray mass of the basilica, surmounted by its dome, is impressive enough. When the outlines of the dome appear out of the night and float in the darkness above the Eternal City, in an atmosphere alive with the iridescence of their own red glow, words fail to describe the effect."

Some might argue that the ceremonies in Rome, in May 1925, were all a bit much for Thérèse of Lisieux – a simple girl, with her simple way. Her message, after all, was the antithesis of the pomp and circumstance witnessed that day. Either way, in 1925, she became a saint for her times – at odds with many of the saints who had gone before her. Perhaps that is partly why so many had flocked to Rome, why so many others had wanted to be there, and why the canonisation was regarded as one of the most moving and special ever held at St. Peter's.

Many Irish people were first introduced to the Little Flower through a silent film that was screened in the mid-1920s.

The arrival, in October 1926, of the French black-and-white silent film, *The Vow*, had Irish audiences packing cinemas and critics singing its praises. The film opened in the Grand Central, in Dublin's O'Connell Street, with its 800 plush seats and vertigo-inducing balcony. The venue certainly was a picture palace of note.

The Grand Central's advertising promised filmgoers a rare treat – a film about a miracle of St. Thérèse, "The Girl Saint of Lisieux." The film was, it said, a "story of love and humble life," "a poem of suffering" and "a song of hope for the hearts of the world." As if that wasn't enough, the publicity went on to declare: "This story is dedicated to womanhood, but men will enjoy it – and cry."

The promotion blitz worked. Crowds packed the Dublin cinema and the reviews were ecstatic. Phrases such as "wonderful French masterpiece," "remarkable film" and "artistic treat of the season" were soon cropping up in the press. The film went on national release, appearing in Cork, Drogheda, Longford and Sligo, among many other cinematic centres, even though their numbers were limited at the time.

Like other films of its era, the plot was complex, to say the least. It was essentially a love story, with the Little Flower at its core. In order to save her father from ruin, the heroine reluctantly accepts that she must marry a man she does not love. Turning to the Little Flower for help, she visits Lisieux and becomes enthralled by the future saint. Eventually, she vows to join the Carmelites and is saved from her dreaded marriage.

Although she meets another young man, who this time she loves, she feels bound by her vow. Illness follows, but she recovers after experiencing a vision of the Little Flower. Not only does the vision restore the heroine's health, but the saint advises her to marry the man she loves. This she does and, as we might have guessed, she and her husband find happiness ever after.

Whether men did cry or not, as the cinema posters promised, we do not know. What we do know is that despite the French cast – with Janine Lequesne playing Thérèse and Simone Vaudry playing the heroine, along with direction from Frenchman Georges Pallu – the critics loved it. One reviewer, in *The Cork Examiner*, referred to the "skill" of the production, "noteworthy" photography and "excellent standard" of acting. Another critic, writing in *The Connacht Tribune*, remarked: "Even if it were only to witness the scenes at Lisieux, this film is well worth seeing."

A further reviewer, writing in the *Evening Herald*, also praised the scenes at Lisieux, while adding: "The picture is treated with great beauty of detail, and follows the life of the girl saint with absolute accuracy: it is produced on the highest artistic lines which we are beginning to associate with the best productions of France. The same people gave us *The Miracle of Lourdes* and *Les Miserables*, and they have gone one better this time."

After its enormous success in Dublin, *The Vow* went on national tour, battling against other megastars and films of 1926, including Greta Garbo in *The Temptress*, Rudolph Valentino in *The Son of the Sheik*, Lionel Barrymore in *The Bells*, Douglas Fairbanks in *The Black Pirate* and Buster Keaton in *The General*. Despite the stiff competition, *The Vow* packed them in. It also did well in France, where it was titled *La Rose Effeuillée*, and performed well in Austria, Brazil, Greece and Portugal, among other countries, under various local titles.

Within a year – by 1927 – the death knell of silent films was signalled by the release of the first sound film, *The Jazz Singer*. Soon, silent movies were being replaced by "talkies" with their recorded voices. The cast and crew of *The Vow*, however, were not finished yet. Janine Lequesne, who played Thérèse, went on to further success as an actress, as did Simone Vaudry, who played the heroine. The director, Georges Pallu, also made numerous other films before his death in 1948.

There would be many, many more films about Thérèse in the years ahead, including *Thérèse Martin* (1938), *Miracle of St. Thérèse* (1952) and the simply-named *Thérèse* (1986). Few had the impact of that flickering, quivering black-and-white silent production, *The Vow*, which so charmed and enchanted audiences back in the mid-1920s. Its genre – the silent movie – may have been facing annihilation but, as the *Evening Herald* remarked, that particular production certainly had an impact.

"This film marks an epoch in the history of the kinematograph," the *Evening Herald* review concluded. "It proves that the silver sheet can be made the medium of raising, instead of lowering, the morals of the people, and that screen entertainment can be sane without being stodgy, romantic without being revolting. It also proves that if we search the markets on this side of the Atlantic we can unearth works surpassing in quality of theme and excellence of production those to which we are being introduced from the far west....If you see this picture you will come away feeling that there is something in this world greater than the world itself."

An Irish-American priest was granted a rare visit to the inner Carmel in the late 1920s. He later reported on the sights he witnessed.

In 1888, aged 15, Thérèse passed through the cloister door at the Carmel in Lisieux. She knew that the door marked the boundary between the life she once knew and a life of isolation devoted to God. It was a barrier through which no outsider entered, and no sister departed. It was no surprise, then, that she would later comment on how she felt as she passed through the door: "My heart became so violent that I wondered if I were going to die."

Almost four decades later, Fr. Albert Dolan, a prominent Irish-American devotee of Thérèse and prolific author, attempted to retrace the footsteps of the Little Flower. He had tried for some time to get permission to pass through the cloister door, and see beyond it, but access was always denied. The Vatican said there was nothing they could do. Even Mother Agnès, the prioress, whom he knew, explained that entry was impossible.

There was one glimmer of hope, Mother Agnès explained. A cardinal could enter, and a priest could accompany him during his visit. The problem facing Fr. Dolan was how to find a cardinal with time on his hands and a helpful disposition. Perhaps the fact that Fr. Dolan had founded the American Society of St. Thérèse and a shrine to the Little Flower in New

Jersey may have helped. Or maybe it was that Cardinal Dubois of Paris had once been his guest in America. Either way, the cardinal agreed to accompany him on a visit.

Standing before the heavy door, the two visitors waited until the bolt was pulled back and the portal creaked open on its hinges. Confronting them was an extraordinary sight. Kneeling in wait were all the nuns of the Carmel. They were on their knees, anticipating the cardinal's arrival and hoping for his blessing. He willingly obliged.

They then met Mother Agnès, whose face was revealed for the first time to Father Dolan; on previous visits he had spoken to her through a grille. He complied with her request not to describe her appearance, although he later said that, in manner and looks, she was everything you would expect of a sister and second mother to St. Thérèse.

Their first port of call was the infirmary. It was there that Thérèse had suffered her final agonies in the lead-up to her death. Its walls seemed to reverberate to the sounds of all that was said and done as she lay dying. Famous words had been spoken there. She had once whispered from her bed: "I will let fall from heaven a shower of roses, I will spend my heaven doing good upon earth."

Other notable words had been uttered there, too. One day, a nun asked Thérèse if, after death, she would look down on her sisters from heaven. "No, I will come down," she had promised. Another day, while in severe pain, she had repeated over and over: "If people only knew how necessary it is to pray for the dying." This last remark reflected not only the intense agonies she was suffering, but her belief that prayers were necessary for those on the edge of death.

Fr. Dolan and Cardinal Dubois said Mass in the infirmary. We can only imagine Fr. Dolan's surprise when, lost in the rites and solemnity of the sacrament, he turned during the "dominus vobiscums" – those ancient salutations where the congregation are told "The Lord be with you" and they respond with "And also with you" – and was confronted by a strange sight.

Instead of facing a regular church congregation, or even a congregation of nuns, in front of him was a "little white bed, so old, so poor and yet so rich, so rich in having been the place of repose of our saint." On another occasion, during the "orate fratres" – the exhortation where the congregation is asked to pray that "my sacrifice and yours may be acceptable to God" – his vestments touched her bed. He felt she was there, watching him.

Fr. Dolan also visited Thérèse's cell. He entered the small room, with no fireplace and a bed as hard as wood. "It was on this hard bed of boards that the child accustomed to the comfort of her father's home had slept," he later wrote. The cell had also been fondly recalled by Thérèse as death approached. When Mother Agnès, her sister, had mentioned how sad she would be seeing the cell after Thérèse was gone, the Little Flower had responded that a great deal of her happiness was acquired in that cell.

Perhaps of all the locations witnessed during Fr. Dolan's visit, the one that stood out most was the garden. It was there that her autobiography had been written. There, too, was the tree under which she sat in her wheelchair, writing the last pages of her book. The garden was bordered by simple brick pillars and a walkway of flagstones which Thérèse had swept so often with her broom. The walkway, Fr. Dolan reflected, was an "isle of peace", a corner of paradise where one's only thoughts could have been of eternity.

Following his visit to the Carmel, Fr. Dolan returned to America, where he continued to work as a priest. He became a prodigious author, publishing 53 books. He also delivered talks about his visit to the Carmel, which were held at the National Shrine of the Little Flower in Chicago. These talks were later published as part of a book, *Collected Little Flower Works*.

Drawing from his Irish background, Fr. Dolan additionally set up an organisation called the Matt Talbot Legion, which helped alcoholics. He achieved all this – including his many visits to Lisieux – in the space of 57 years. He died in 1951, a young man, no doubt still recalling that special visit to the Carmel where, as he once put it, his soul and the soul of Cardinal Dubois had been placed "under the spell of the charm of the cloister and filled with all that we had seen and heard there."

The Irish media and general public were transfixed by an Anglican preacher's conversion to Catholicism in 1929. The conversion was attributed to Thérèse of Lisieux.

Back in the 1920s, nothing caught the Irish public's attention more than a conversion to Catholicism. That anyone would abandon an "alien" faith and switch to the "true" faith was significant news. Interest grew exponentially if the person was an English-born Anglican preacher whose conversion was brought about by the Little Flower.

That was exactly the scenario presenting itself in the case of Rev. Vernon Johnson. Educated at Charterhouse – the prestigious English public school – he was ordained to the Anglican ministry after studying at both Oxford University and Ely Theological College. During his years of service, he acquired a reputation as "one of the greatest public orators of the day." His career path changed in 1929 when he converted to Catholicism. The change was all down to Thérèse of Lisieux.

The seeds of his conversion were sown in late autumn 1924, when he was sent to an Anglican convent on retreat. While there, the reverend mother presented him with a copy of the Little Flower's autobiography. He had no interest in reading it, believing it was just another Catholic ruse to drum up devotion and support.

Back in his room, he decided to give the book a try. Initially, he found it boring but quickly changed his mind. It was long after midnight before he finally put it down. As he remarked in his book, *One Lord – One Faith*, published in 1929, Thérèse's autobiography "moved my whole being as no other piece of writing has ever done."

He continued: "Here was someone who had loved Our Lord to a degree beyond anything I had met before: a love as strong as that of the martyrs of old, and yet with the delicacy and tenderness of a little child, so delicate and tender that one almost fails to realise the furnace in which that love was so wonderfully refined."

He was soon on his way to Lisieux. His first visit, by a strange quirk of fate, was on the day of Thérèse's canonisation. The garish decorations repulsed him; he deemed them to be artificial and sentimental. He was more interested in objects associated with her life: her spoon and fork, sandals, needle case, artificial flowers she had made as she awaited death, pictures she had painted. Seeing these objects moved him.

He also visited her home, where he was deeply touched seeing the fireplace next to which she placed her shoes on Christmas Eve, and the room where she ate her last meal before entering the Carmel. At one stage, he had a conversation with a woman who had gone to school with Thérèse and had often sat beside her in class. He also visited the Little Flower's grave.

Through a chance introduction, he was given a private audience with Mother Agnès. It was a short interview, spoken at the grille, with a white curtain in between. He listened to the same voice Thérèse had heard years before, kneeling at the same spot where she had knelt in floods of tears, talking to her "little Mother Pauline." It was the high point of a magical and memorable visit, which he later described as "a spiritual experience unlike anything I had ever known in my life before."

A second visit followed in 1926. By this time, not only was Johnson questioning the basic tenets of Anglicanism but he was also examining the doctrines and beliefs of the Catholic Church. Anglicanism, he concluded, had lost its way. It had become, he believed, like a debating society, discussing issues rather than teaching eternal truths. It lacked authority. By comparison, there was a sense of unity and authority to Catholicism, all down to the central role of the pope.

Johnson's formal conversion to Catholicism, which took place in 1929, was well-received in Ireland. The press loved the story. "Anglican Preacher's Conversion," was a typical headline. The reaction was equally enthusiastic when, later that year, he brought out his book, *One Lord – One Faith*, detailing why he took his momentous step. "A remarkable book," one critic called it.

Inspired by his newfound popularity, Fr. Johnson was soon visiting Ireland, with Cork City Hall being his first port of call. His lecture there – titled *The Little Flower, St. Thérèse of Lisieux* – was delivered to a "large audience," reports noted. Holding Thérèse up as a model for the world, he decried not only the rise in materialism but the loss of both faith and the love of God.

"Sweeping across the world today is the passionate desire to be happy," he said in his distinctive oratorical style. "But are the people happy? They have only got to look at themselves to see." By way of contrast, he argued, was the message of Thérèse. She was crying to the pagan world that it was following a false scent. Her message was simple, he thundered: "There is only one thing can make you happy – the knowledge that you are your Father's child."

Not only did the audience love it in Cork, but later that year Fr. Johnson delivered a similar lecture to a packed Gaiety Theatre in Dublin. Not surprisingly, he was invited back to Ireland time and again. Three thousand people attended a novena he conducted in Dublin in honour of St. Thérèse. People also bought his many books, a large number of them devoted to themes concerning the Little Flower.

Fr. Johnson also built a successful profile in Britain, where he ended up becoming Catholic chaplain to Oxford University. It must have seemed a curious appointment to many people, given that he had once studied there as an Anglican. His other duties included working with the Catholic Missionary Society and acting as chaplain of Sudbury Hill convent, not to mention his efforts on behalf of St. Thérèse – all of which would never have happened but for a copy of the Little Flower's book being passed to him by a nun in 1924.

An Irish-American priest and devotee of St. Thérèse battled on behalf of coloured people in 1920s New York. The cause for his canonisation was initiated by the Brooklyn diocese in 2008.

In 1928, an orphanage for black children in Long Island, New York, was burnt to the ground. The culprits were the Ku Klux Klan who, along with many white residents, didn't want coloured children living in the neighbourhood. Spotting that the orphanage was being rebuilt, the Klan watched and waited and, after it rose from the ashes, they burnt it to cinders once more.

Within months, yet another structure sprung up. Just who wasn't getting the message, the Klan wondered? It certainly wasn't the local white residents; nor was it the diocesan senior clergy; nor, indeed, was it any established politician. Instead, it was an ordinary priest who was determined not to let his flock down. Clearly, this dogged cleric couldn't be stopped.

The priest was Fr. Bernard J. Quinn, who had been born to Irish immigrant parents in nearby Newark, New Jersey. The family he came from was poor, with his father Bernard and mother Sarah raising their seven children on a longshoreman's meagre wages. Perhaps it was this humble upbringing that made Fr. Bernard aware of the misfortunes of others. He certainly was conscious of the deprivation suffered by those who didn't have white skin.

Fr. Quinn's greatest compassion was reserved for young coloured orphans who had no families of their own and no homes to go to. Outraged by the burning of the orphanage, he wrote: "It is surely difficult to understand how anybody could refuse a bed and shelter to a helpless, homeless child no matter what its colour or creed might be." He went even further, facing down those who threatened him or those in his care. "I would willingly shed to the last drop my life's blood for the least among you," he told his parishioners.

To Fr. Quinn, everyone mattered. Irrespective of how small, unimportant or insignificant people were, they deserved care and protection. Whatever their race, colour or creed, they were important in the eyes of God. If this philosophy sounds familiar, that's because it is. It comes from the love of Fr. Quinn's life, the person whose little way inspired him – St. Thérèse of Lisieux.

Fr. Quinn felt close to Thérèse and had visited her home in Alençon and the Carmel in Lisieux. He did so at the end of World War I, when as a soldier-priest with the United States Army he had travelled the 50 km from where he was stationed to the place of the Little Flower's birth. Having read *Story of a Soul*, he had, he said, fallen "head over heels" for the future saint.

At the Carmel, he met Mother Agnès – Thérèse's sister, Pauline – whom he blessed and spoke to at length. She was clearly impressed by her visitor and, before he departed, presented him with a precious relic – strands of the Little Flower's hair cut during the ceremony when she was being clothed in the Carmelite habit. He never forgot the importance of that gift.

Buoyed by his devotion to Thérèse, Fr. Quinn returned to New York where he set about caring for the growing population of coloured people in the Brooklyn diocese. Their numbers had expanded due to the increased mechanisation of farming in the American south, leading to mass migration northwards, and an influx of migrants from the Caribbean.

In 1921, he established the first church for black Catholics in New York. It was an enormous success, resulting in the conversion of many coloured people to Catholicism. An astonishing 10,000 parishioners attended its weekly St. Thérèse novenas. Among those who emerged from its parochial school was the singer and activist Lena Horne.

He then set about his orphanage project, which, despite the keen attentions of the Klan, opened successfully in 1930. Not surprisingly, it too reflected Fr. Quinn's devotion to Thérèse. Called the Little Flower House of Providence for Homeless Coloured Children, it was placed under the saint's protection.

Known as a warm, humorous, approachable man, Fr. Bernard – or "Barney" as he was known to his friends – never hid from condemnation or controversy, especially concerning his coloured parishioners. He was always willing to be photographed with his coloured congregation. These black-and-white snapshots – many of which survive to this day – must have enraged his detractors back in the racially-charged 1920s. It was no wonder that his parishioners trusted him and loved him to bits.

From the way he tackled setbacks, it was clear that Fr. Quinn had learned well from Thérèse. All his ordeals and troubles he handled with grace and composure. He once commented on how Thérèse had dealt with her trials, remarking: "Picture this child enduring all this with a calm and peaceful resignation.... even with gratitude. Once, when one of her sisters asked her how it was that none of these things seemed to disturb her, she replied: 'It was not always so, but I have learned to forget self, and since then I am at peace.'"

He also practised her little way. No greater mistake could be made, he argued, than to confuse enormous sacrifices and wonderful mortifications with sanctity and sainthood. Thérèse, he said, took a more enlightened view, doing "the common things of life uncommonly well. Herein lay the secret of her sanctity. Herein lies for us the happy thought that we, too, will become saints of God if we but perform the ordinary duties of our state in life extraordinarily well."

Fr. Quinn certainly exhibited all the attributes of a "saint of God" up to the time of his death on 7 April 1940. He died young – aged just 52 – from a painful carcinoma. Thousands of mourners thronged the streets to wish him goodbye. The huge turnout was no surprise. After all, at a time when one anti-black priest in New York was declaring that "negroes" should be excluded from his church if "they become numerous," he had championed their cause.

Fr. Quinn's position was simple and clear: "It seems to me that no church can exclude anyone and still keep its Christian ideals." Anyone can go anyplace to worship, he argued. And everyone mattered in the eyes of God. It was a philosophy which, although it no doubt sprung from his heart, owed much to a saint whose life was lived far from the racially-divided battleground of Brooklyn, New York.

What follows is the story of how, in 1932, an Irish-American cardinal masterminded one of the most famous pilgrimages in history. It involved a visit to Ireland's Eucharistic Congress and an historic blessing at Lisieux.

On Tuesday, 21 June 1932, the majestic Red Star liner, *SS Lapland*, sailed into Dublin Bay and anchored off the port of Dun Laoghaire. The ship carried a massive complement of 1,200 American pilgrims, 500 of them from Philadelphia, who were on the voyage of a lifetime. Most were of Irish parentage and were travelling for the first time to the land of their fathers. Emotions ran so high that loud cheers rang out aboard ship when Irish shores were first sighted.

"Do not mind them if they seem to do funny things," one of the priests on board told waiting reporters. "Most of them have been looking forward to this all their lives and they are bent on enjoying themselves when they land in Ireland." It was pointed out that even more would have travelled but for America's infamous Wall Street Crash. "Many men who had saved all their lives to come to Ireland for the congress had lost their all in the crash and now had their backs to the wall," the *Irish Independent* pointed out.

The visit to Ireland formed only part of that pilgrimage in 1932. Five days after its arrival, the liner set sail for Le Havre. From there, many of the pilgrims travelled to Lisieux, where they attended an historic blessing at the Basilica of St. Thérèse, which had been under construction for some time. Even that didn't end their tour – they then travelled to Rome, following which they returned to their homes in America.

It took a man of vision to organise an adventure as daring as that famous American pilgrimage of 1932. That man was Cardinal Dennis Joseph Dougherty, Archbishop of Philadelphia. His parents were Irish and had emigrated from County Mayo to escape the poverty prevailing in their home country. It wasn't all plain sailing in America, where his father had to support his wife and ten children out of a coalminer's wages.

The young Dennis – who the parents nicknamed "Dinny" – turned out to be a brilliant scholar and was ordained to the priesthood in 1890. He quickly rose through Church ranks, becoming a bishop, archbishop and cardinal. Appointed

Archbishop of Philadelphia in 1918, he was highly regarded by Rome and had access to the Vatican at the highest level. Nothing fazed him, not even organising a pilgrimage on a world-famous transatlantic liner that had once hosted the honeymooning actors Douglas Fairbanks and Mary Pickford.

Along with the other pilgrims, he had used the *SS Lapland* as a "floating hotel" during the 1932 Eucharistic Congress, which was attended by over a million people in Dublin's Phoenix Park. One of those who visited him on board the ship was Éamon de Valera, who had a dual purpose in mind. Not only did he want to thank Dougherty for his role in raising $100,000 to support Ireland's struggle for independence, but he also wished to show him the compartment in which he had stowed away when he first made his way to America as a fugitive. This he duly did.

"The outstanding impression," Cardinal Dougherty said at the conclusion of the congress, "was the wonderful outburst of Catholic faith and devotion. I have never seen the equal of it in any other part of the world. This will be a memorable day in the history of Ireland, and will probably be told by one generation to its successor for many years to come." Then, on Sunday, 26 June, the *SS Lapland* departed Dun Laoghaire and headed for France en route to Rome.

There was every reason for Cardinal Dougherty to look forward to his visit to Lisieux. Although he was a man of big ideas and equally big achievements, he was a huge fan of Thérèse's little way. He had first come across her in 1912, when he was asked by a lay worker in a convent to buy a copy of *Story of a Soul*, written by the Little Flower.

"Who is the Little Flower?" he asked, never having heard of her before. "Why, don't you know of the Little Flower?" the woman replied. "She was a Carmelite nun, who died in the odour of sanctity not many years ago." He duly bought the book, returned to the priest's house in which he was staying and, as he later put it: "Needless to say, it thrilled me."

The following year, 1913, he visited the Carmel in Lisieux, where he met Mother Agnès, sister of Thérèse. He later recollected: "I was admitted into the cloister, where I found four nuns kneeling just inside the door, ready to receive me. As soon as I entered they threw back the long black veils, which screened their faces and bodies, arose and greeted me. My first words were: 'Which is Mother Agnès?' The smallest of the four smilingly replied: 'I am Mother Agnès'; after a little pause she added: 'The Little Flower was taller than I.'"

On that occasion, Dougherty remained in Lisieux for three days and became intimately acquainted with the life of Thérèse. "I first visited the Little Flower's cell," he said. "In leaving the cell, I noticed a thick piece of glass on the jamb of the door. Mother Agnès called my attention to writing beneath it. I examined it and found under the glass the word 'Thérèse' scratched there with a nail by the hand of the Little Flower."

Captivated by the future saint, Dougherty paid further visits to Lisieux and was present at the Little Flower's beatification in 1923. Known for his fundraising skills, he was appointed to the Committee of Patronage set up to aid in the construction of the new Basilica of St. Thérèse. It was in that role, and because of his significance as a churchman, that he was invited to consecrate the first part of the new basilica in 1932.

The event was a colourful one, involving the inauguration of the crypt and the front entrance to the structure. No less than 60 bishops were present, with Masses and benediction being held to commemorate the occasion. Lisieux was packed with pilgrims pouring in from near and far, among them the delegation from Philadelphia.

The streets were "a constant scene of animation and colour and stir," one newspaper noted. There was a great procession, the report added, which "progressed through the principal streets until it reached the flank of the hill, on which can already be seen the foundation of the noble cathedral which is to be erected to the glory of the saint."

The ceremony wasn't, by any means, the first or last that would be held at the basilica. As far back as 1929, the laying of the foundation stone had been commemorated, and in 1937 the basilica was formally blessed by the papal legate Cardinal Pacelli, who would later become Pope Pius XII. Because of World War II, it would take until 1954 for the structure to be finally completed.

Sadly, Cardinal Dougherty was unable to see the finished product. He died in 1951, aged 85, from the effects of a stroke. His loss to the Church was a great one, summed up by remarks made in *The Irish Press*: "His ability as an administrator, his capacity as a scholar, his missionary zeal, his profound simplicity and sympathy, all conspire to make this great churchman a truly remarkable man." Although his contribution to, and support for, the Basilica of St. Thérèse was one of his lasting legacies, he wasn't the only person of Irish lineage to contribute to the project, as we are about to see.

In the late 1930s, a Dublin-born priest almost singlehandedly raised the money to create an Irish side chapel in the Basilica of St. Thérèse at Lisieux.

Throughout 1936 and part of 1937, Irish families who were lucky enough to own radio sets could participate in Masses beamed from the Carmelite monastery in Lisieux. Depending on weather and general atmospheric conditions, these "wireless pilgrimages", as they were called, enabled radio owners to feel as if they were sitting in the same tiny chapel that Thérèse had once known so well. The saint's sisters also attended the Masses that listeners were tuned into on their sets.

Transmissions took place on the first Thursday of each month, courtesy of Radio Normandie. Operating out of the small French coastal town of Fécamp, this commercial radio station was proving something of a hit with audiences in Ireland. Broadcasting light music and popular music, along with operas and operettas, the station's output appealed to Irish listening tastes. "I daresay that many of you have listened to the delightful concerts which come from Radio Normandie every Sunday," one Irish radio commentator noted in his newspaper column.

Matters took a new twist when, from 1938 – 1939, not only did broadcasts from Lisieux continue, but an Irish priest issued accompanying appeals for donations towards the building of an Irish side chapel in the town's new basilica. His name was Fr. John Power, a Dubliner, who along with two of his brothers, worked as priests in England. Because of his radio appeals, he became known as the "Irish Broadcaster" and was soon a well-known and popular figure in media circles.

Fr. Power had an interesting history. Having left Ireland for England, he was sent as parish priest to the inner-city area of Saltley, Birmingham. At the time, Saltley had no church or school; indeed, it had a debt of £8,000 on the plot of land where Masses were held in an old army hut. Placing his trust in God, he travelled to Lisieux, where he met Mother Agnès. She promised to pray to her sister for help with his work in Saltley.

Fr. Power ended up erecting over £100,000 worth of Church property in his parish, including one of the largest schools in England. Considerable sums of money were sent from Ireland following his appeals for support. Among the contributors, he noted, were "the mothers of five of the men who were executed in Dublin in 1916, and numerous Irish mothers whose sons were killed in the Anglo-Irish war." It is interesting to note how, at a time of so much hardship, Irish people were sending such huge sums of money abroad.

As a gesture of thanks to Lisieux, Fr. Power proposed that he would raise money to build an Irish chapel in the Basilica of St. Thérèse, which was being decorated and finished off at the time. The plan was that a series of side chapels would be built within the structure, each of which would be sponsored by people from specific countries – mostly the prominent Catholic nations of the world.

Writing in the *Irish Independent*, in late 1938, Fr. Power explained the plan: "The great Basilica of St. Thérèse at Lisieux, built to accommodate the ever increasing thousands who can no longer find accommodation in the chapel of the Carmelite convent, contains 16 huge side chapels, each almost as large as an ordinary size parish church....The ecclesiastical authority at

Lisieux are keenly anxious that the great Irish Catholic nation should adopt and dedicate one of the chapels to our national patron St. Patrick. The cost will be roughly about £1,000 which is not a great deal for Catholic Ireland."

The idea was to embellish and decorate the Irish chapel with materials from Ireland, including Connemara green marble and the black marble of Kilkenny. The arms of Ireland would be worked in golden mosaics, as would the arms of the four provinces and chief towns and cities. Adept at using words, this project, Fr. Power declared, would not only provide Irish people with "a link between the living and the dead" but would become "a national monument of their faith."

He also utilised the Irish media to great effect. He once took out a newspaper advertisement demanding of the Irish nation: "Since our last appeal, the Catholics of two neighbouring Protestant nations have given national chapels at Lisieux – Is Catholic Ireland to be outdone by Protestant lands?" The correct address to which donations were to be sent, "by registered post", was then listed.

Not only did Fr. Power raise the £1,000 he had initially planned, but the figure rose to more than £5,000 by the early summer of 1939. It was an astonishing sum of money for its time. By then, the Irish chapel was up and running, with its first Mass celebrated by Fr. Power in July of that year. Over the altar hung a tricolour inscribed in Irish: "From the people of Ireland to Sainte Thérèse, 1925," with the date referring to the year of her canonisation.

That summer, more than 500 pilgrims from Ireland took part in ceremonies offering thanksgiving for Ireland's contribution to the chapel. They marched in procession to the basilica, carrying banners representing St. Patrick and St. Brigid. Some 2,000 children formed a guard of honour outside the basilica door. An Irish choir was present.

Fr. Power, in yet another broadcast, which was transmitted that day, thanked the Irish people who had contributed to the project. He said: "You have just heard solemn High Mass in the crypt of the great Basilica of St. Thérèse at Lisieux sung by Irish priests for the first Irish pilgrimage to come here in thanksgiving for the success of our radio appeal to Ireland for funds to build the Irish chapel; and this morning, in the name of Mother Agnès and the Carmelites of Lisieux, and in my own name, I thank you for your magnificent response."

Unable to resist the temptation, this remarkable priest then went on to explain that, although the Irish chapel was completed, "millions of francs were still required" for final work on the basilica itself. He said he hoped that Irish people would "continue their help." It is hard to credit but, within two years, the Irish contribution had grown to a staggering £7,000! Lisieux would never see the likes of Fr. Power's fundraising skills again!

Taoiseach and future President of Ireland, Éamon de Valera, visited Lisieux in 1938, seeking help from the Little Flower.

There is a wonderful photograph of Taoiseach Éamon de Valera at Lisieux on 9 September 1938. It is a relaxed picture, reflecting the unofficial, private nature of the visit. In the centre stands the towering de Valera, who is accompanied, left and right, by his daughters Máirín and Emer, his aide-de-camp Captain Seán

Brennan and Denis McDonald of the Department of External Affairs.

De Valera was in Lisieux for a reason – seeking help for his failing eyesight. The problem dated back to his imprisonment following the 1916 Rising, when he read almost endlessly under unsuitable conditions. For years, documents for his perusal had to be written on a special typewriter containing large letters. Shaded lamps also had to be fitted behind his seat in the Dáil and in his private office to relieve the strain on his eyes.

In 1936, two years before the Lisieux visit, de Valera had travelled to Zurich for an operation performed by the famous Swiss eye surgeon, Professor Dr. Alfred Vogt. Dublin being a small city, he had also been spotted seeking help for his problem. As early as 1932, a journalist with *The Cork Examiner* – who was himself seeking treatment – bumped into de Valera in a well-known Dublin optician's waiting room. De Valera "laughed heartily," knowing he had been rumbled.

The Lisieux visit was an add-on to a trip to Geneva where de Valera was scheduled to attend the Assembly of the League of Nations in September 1938. He departed Dun Laoghaire on the *Cambria*, stayed at the Grosvenor Hotel in London – where he had meetings with British officials – then took the *Golden Arrow* from Victoria Station to Dover, and from there travelled to Paris and Lisieux.

He eventually arrived at the Carmel at 11.30 am, on Friday, 9 September, where he was received by Mother Agnès, prioress and sister of Thérèse. He proceeded to explain his devotion to the saint. It dated back, he said, to earlier that year, when he and British Prime Minister Neville Chamberlain agreed the terms of the Anglo-Irish Trade Agreement. Complex negotiations surrounded the agreement, which lifted excise duties imposed during the previous five years and also ended British use of Irish ports.

"Just as I was about to undertake these negotiations with representatives of the British Government," he remarked, "I obtained, through the good offices of a priest, a friend of mine, a precious relic of St. Thérèse, and that relic never left me while the parleys continued. At their successful conclusion, I promised to make a pilgrimage to Lisieux." He then showed Mother Agnès the medallion containing the relic along with a volume in Irish of Thérèse's autobiography, which he had brought with him to read on his journey.

He additionally spoke to Mother Agnès about his failing eyesight and asked that she and her fellow sisters pray for a resolution to his problem. His visit over, he returned to Paris, travelled to Geneva where he spent three weeks at the League of Nations, and followed it up with another visit to Dr. Vogt in Zurich. He finally returned to Ireland. By any standards, it was a gruelling schedule.

In the following months, de Valera exchanged letters with Mother Agnès, thanking her for her hospitality and, above all, asking for more prayers. In one of those letters, he spoke of how his consultant seemed anxious and proposed another operation for September 1939. He added: "Meanwhile he expects that my sight will deteriorate and reading become a little more difficult....Please do continue to ask the Little Flower to help if it is God's will so that I may be able to read and do my work efficiently."

There would be no instant miracle for Éamon de Valera, certainly in terms of a cure for his failing eyesight. Instead, in the years ahead, his problem became worse. Eventually, he was forced to spend several months in the Netherlands, where he had six operations, and he was away from Ireland for quite some time.

In other ways, however, his life ahead was miraculous. He continued in politics, both as Taoiseach and later as President of Ireland. He also travelled far and wide, visiting places as distant as India, Australia, New Zealand, Canada and Italy – and that's not including his pilgrimages to various international shrines of Catholic worship.

He was also able to deliver noteworthy speeches, using his memory instead of notes or manuscripts. On one occasion, in May 1964, he spoke before a joint session of the U.S. Congress, without referring to any notes at all. "His thought-provoking, statesman-like speech made a profound impression on his distinguished audience," one political commentator noted. It was said that the atmosphere in the House of Representatives was charged with emotion. Remarkably, when he delivered that speech, he was 81 years of age.

When he died, in August 1975, Éamon de Valera was aged 92 and blind. An estimated 80,000 people filed past his body, which was laid out in the habit of a Carmelite friar at Dublin Castle. They passed by at the rate of more than 3,000 an hour. His body was eventually brought to the Pro-Cathedral, where a Requiem Mass was celebrated, before burial at Glasnevin Cemetery.

We do not know his final thoughts as he lay dying at a convalescent home in Blackrock, County Dublin. What we do know is that, throughout his life, he always remembered his visit to Lisieux. "The recollection will remain with us always," he once remarked in a letter to Mother Agnès. In that letter, he went on to say: "When the hour of my death comes I want you to ask your sister to intercede for me," and he ended with a poignant line – written in French – saying, "I will never forget my visit to the Carmel of Lisieux."

A MODERN-DAY SAINT

An outburst of euphoria greeted the Little Flower's relics during their visit to Ireland in 2001. Up to three million people turned out for the event. The vast number was no surprise as, by then, Thérèse had become one of the most popular saints, standing alongside St. Anthony of Padua, St. Francis of Assisi and St. Pio of Pietrelcina.

A succession of popes had already extolled her virtues. Pope Pius X called her "the greatest saint of modern times." Pope Pius XI declared her "the star of my pontificate." Pope John Paul II referred to her as one of "the great masters of the spirit." Even Padre Pio became a devotee, having read *Story of a Soul*.

New plays, biographies, lectures and press coverage – not to mention the opening of churches and the naming of houses – had copper-fastened her place in Irish culture. It would be safe to say that towards the end of World War II – less than five decades since her death – the Little Flower's name was on everyone's lips.

The survival of the historic Carmel at Lisieux, together with St. Thérèse's childhood home and the basilica in her name, was one of the great miracles of World War II. Irish people were over-joyed at the news.

On the evening of 5 June 1944 – the night before D-Day – a wave of Allied planes bombarded Lisieux. The attack started at eight o'clock; another followed at two o'clock the next morning; a third took place at two o'clock in the afternoon. The town was almost completely destroyed; its buildings set ablaze, its streets filled with rubble. Lisieux could be seen for many miles burning like a blazing torch. The town was a sea of flames for a week.

Some 60 religious were killed in Lisieux that night. Twenty-one nuns died at the Abbey of the Benedictines, where Thérèse had been educated. Thirteen Sisters of the Poor were burned in their asylum. The nuns at the Carmel were in grave danger. As darkness fell, they set out from their cloister and headed for the crypt at the basilica seeking shelter. That crypt became their temporary home.

"The news of the reported destruction of Lisieux made sad reading for thousands of Irish people who have happy memories of the simple, unpretentious little church beside the Carmelite convent made world-famous by its association with the Little Flower," the *Irish Independent* commented, as news filtered through from the front. "After Rome and Lourdes no place was more universally beloved than this blossoming place of the saint."

Although Lisieux was having a quiet war, its fortunes declined dramatically around D-Day. Situated 25 miles from the sea and 112 miles from Paris, it had become a pivot point for the German forces occupying northern France. It was also one of their vital communications centres. Inevitably, the railway station became target number one for the bombers; the area around it was blasted to bits.

With heavy hearts, the nuns of the Carmel – including two of Thérèse's sisters – walked through the carnage and headed for the basilica. As they left the convent, one side of their street was already in flames; following their departure, the flames licked the sanctuary but it was saved when the wind changed direction. They eventually arrived at their destination, where the Red Cross provided beds in the nave of the crypt.

At the basilica, the nuns joined other terrified residents of Lisieux. People living in the wider hinterland had also arrived seeking refuge, believing that the Little Flower's home town would be safe. To their surprise, it was anything but. Now, along with the townsfolk, they either crammed into the basilica or fled to the hills in an effort to escape the relentless onslaught from the air.

Back in the Carmel, the bombs rained down. Eighty-five landed in the interior gardens. Heavy stones and general debris penetrated the structure, especially parts of the roofs and walls. Fearful that priceless relics of Thérèse might be destroyed, priests carried them to the basilica. Both relics and nuns remained there as the land battle for Lisieux began in earnest.

On 22 August, the first Allied tanks, accompanied by combat troops, made their way into Lisieux. The town echoed to the sound of machinegun and rifle fire. "Savage street fighting" was noted in one news report. That night, the Germans retaliated with an artillery bombardment from the nearby hills.

The basilica shook so badly from the bombardment that general absolution was given to all those inside. They didn't know just how much they needed it, as the Allies had received information that 200 German soldiers were also sheltering inside its walls. Their information was accurate, but the soldiers were only terrified fugitives. Miraculously, an order to commence artillery fire was never issued.

Charles Lynch, the Irish-Canadian who provided legendary reports for Reuters news agency, sent graphic dispatches from a tense, terrified Lisieux. Many of them were picked up by the Irish press. "Ours was the first jeep to enter the battered little town," he wrote, "moving in behind the infantry, who are stalking along the streets flushing out snipers. The tanks came along in the rear....I saw a tank which was blocked by rubble from going along a street wheel into the wall of a blasted house and go right through it, disappearing in a cloud of dust in the direction of the enemy."

On 27 August – after 80 days and nights in the crypt – the Carmelite nuns returned to the convent carrying with them the trunk containing the relics of St. Thérèse. Despite the bombs that had rained down near the Carmel, the structure, in the main, had miraculously survived. Although a bomb had fallen in the garden of Les Buissonnets, the building – again, almost miraculously – was untouched.

In the main structure of the basilica, the windows had been blasted and their lead panes were twisted and jagged. The interior of the building was a foot deep in cement dust. But the crypt, which had housed the Carmelite sisters, was, once more, seemingly miraculously free of damage. "Low and intimate, warm in its blue and green mosaics, it is a haven of peace now more than ever before," according to an eyewitness report.

At the beginning of the war – prior to the occupation of France – Mother Agnès, sister of Thérèse, had sent a message from Lisieux hoping "that Ireland may be saved from the horrors of the war." Now, at the war's end, Ireland, in turn, was relieved that the Carmel and other sites linked to Thérèse had been saved from devastation and ruin.

No newspaper summed up Ireland's happiness better than the *Irish Independent*. "Today, after five years of war, the people of Ireland will acknowledge with gratitude the message of Mother Agnès," the newspaper remarked, "and rejoice with her now that her own convent has been saved, and that all the places that St. Thérèse loved are unharmed."

There was still a long way to go in the conflict – the war wouldn't end until September 1945 – but the battleground had moved to the east and all the well-known landmarks linked to Thérèse – the Carmel, the basilica and St. Thérèse's home, Les Buissonnets, had survived as if by the intervention of the Little Flower or by the hand of God.

A play inspired by St. Thérèse kept her name alive in Ireland during World War II.

In 1945, Irish author Francis Stuart attempted to return home from war-torn Germany, where he had delivered numerous broadcasts supporting the Nazi regime. He didn't make it back. Instead, he was arrested and detained by Allied troops. He only reached Dublin in 1958. By then, although infamous for his role during the war, Stuart hadn't been forgotten – instead, he was fondly recalled for a remarkable play which had turned heads in Dublin at the height of the global conflict.

Sold-out signs had accompanied the opening night of Stuart's play, *Strange Guest*, at Dublin's Abbey Theatre, on 9 December 1940. The audience, pre-show, must have wondered what was in store. They got what the *Sunday Independent* promised in a preview would be "a commentary on the moral and social life of a modern family," centred on the arrival in their midst of a nun meant to be the Little Flower.

The plot was simple. The saintly nun – St. Thérèse – seeks shelter with a wealthy country family after her religious community has been disbanded. Her goal is to set up a new community as soon as she possibly can. The dilemma is: where will the funds come from?

Into the picture steps another house guest – a jockey – who offers the nun an opportunity to invest her community's money in a forthcoming race. The jockey knows that his own horse – the favourite – will win, but the odds will be insufficient to generate worthwhile returns. His solution is simple – place the nun's money on an outsider, pull his own horse in the race, thereby making a fortune for the nun. Although he broke his leg in the process, he was cured by what else....a miracle!

The play was a huge success. Greeted by "enthusiastic applause" at its conclusion, it received lavish praise from the critics. "Rarely has there been produced a play of such originality and distinction," declared the *Evening Herald*. "One of the most notable plays produced in recent years," trumpeted the *Sunday Independent*. "A remarkable contribution has been made to the Abbey repertoire," *The Irish Press* added.

Actress Ria Mooney's performance as the nun was singled out by the *Evening Herald*. "The central character is so sensitively drawn," the newspaper remarked. "Like Joan of Arc, she is without guile and insists on speaking her mind. Her very artlessness is a shield on which the agnostic arguments of her hosts and their friends grow blunt." Her performance, the critic said, was "one of her finest in a distinguished career."

The *Irish Independent* also highlighted Mooney, praising her "superb acting" and for having "presented us with an intensely interesting human picture of the mystic." This latter review perceptively remarked that the central character – just like Thérèse – had "a quiet gentle way of doing what she wanted to do" with "supreme confidence in her destiny to achieve great things as a Servant of God."

The other central character – the jockey – was played by Joe Linnane, presenter of *Question Time* on Radio Éireann. He, too, received rave reviews. "The part was so ably played," one critic noted, "that one was tempted to scrutinise the programme so as to ascertain his real identity." Other critics wrote that his performance was "a joy," "lively and witty" and that he played his role "with a sensitive touch that made one see the emotion beneath the toughness."

Following several curtain calls, Iseult Stuart – the author's wife – addressed the audience. She was well qualified to do so, being the daughter of Maud Gonne, the Irish revolutionary, actress and muse of poet William Butler Yeats. She also, of course, knew Stuart's writing methods, having been involved with him since 1920, although at the time of the play their marriage was falling apart.

Speaking to the audience, Iseult described her husband's "intense admiration" for St. Thérèse, prompting him to recognise the "dramatic possibilities" of bringing the great mystic into the presence of ordinary people in a private house. That it was Iseult – and not her husband – who was speaking from the stage, disappointed some, most notably a regional newspaper reviewer who complained that it was "an innovation which it is to be hoped the Abbey won't continue."

Perhaps that newspaperman, as he left the theatre, might have wondered why the playwright – Francis Stuart – wasn't there. Had he listened very, very carefully, he might have figured out the answer. For weeks now, German bombs had been raining down on British cities, dropping their loads on London, Coventry, Birmingham and Liverpool, the latter being little more than 100 miles away. Winds permitting, the sounds of almost 7,000 tons of German bombs being dropped could be heard in Dublin – a city, in many other respects, a world away.

This was wartime Europe and, when the play was premiered, Francis Stuart was no longer in Ireland but living in Germany, where he worked at Berlin University. There he remained until the end of the war, having left his wife behind. Initially an admirer of Hitler, he believed a victory for Germany would result in a united Ireland. He ended up making more than 100 broadcasts to Ireland on German radio, before being interned by the Allies at the war's conclusion.

Although born into an Ulster Unionist family, Stuart had converted to Catholicism and read the Gospels, out of which he got "a lot of comfort and inspiration," as he put it. He was also "very attracted to Thérèse of Lisieux," finding her "a pious little creature," he said. Not only did she feature elsewhere in his works – mostly controversially – but his second wife, Gertrude, who was German, was also a committed devotee. "Yes, I love St. Thérèse," she once said. "It was her loving patience with animals and nature in general that first attracted me to her."

Owing to its popularity, *Strange Guest* had an extended run at the Abbey Theatre in late 1940, continuing over Christmas and into the New Year. The Abbey Players performed it on Radio Éireann in February 1942. The play also had a revival in August of that year, at a time when vicious fighting was being reported near Stalingrad, with huge casualties being inflicted on the Germans.

It was for the 1940 – 1941 production, however, that the play was recalled during the years of World War II. As one newspaper critic remarked, it showed it was possible to "mix holiness and humour" with "faith and the world of common things." Above all, it convincingly highlighted the "simplicity and sincerity" of the Little Flower – attributes that the critic argued "were the outstanding qualities of the nun herself." That alone, he concluded, made it a play with a large vision, deserving a large appreciation.

Gramophone recitals became popular in Limerick during the 1950s. They were inspired by St. Thérèse and received support from the Carmel in Lisieux.

Anyone passing Limerick's Little Flower Hall in the 1950s would have been stunned by the sounds seeping through its windows and doors. They might have caught snatches of a Brahms concerto, a Chopin waltz, Rossini's *William Tell Overture*, or a couple of Handel's arias sung by Kathleen Ferrier. The source of their surprise was what was referred to by enthusiasts in Limerick as a "Feast of Music" session.

The sessions were held twice weekly at the Little Flower Hall, Dominick Street, under the supervision of the music-mad Dominican Fr. Harry Hunt. The idea was simple – the best of classical recordings would be played on the finest equipment, to an assembled audience, and all for the entry fee of a shilling.

From their inception, at the beginning of 1952, all walks of life attended the events.

What was little-known was the role of St. Thérèse in the novel venture. Not only had Fr. Hunt named the hall in her honour, but the sessions were held under her protection and had the blessing of her sister at the Carmel in Lisieux. Sr. Geneviève – who was Thérèse's sister, Céline – was the person who sent the blessing in May 1952.

On hearing about the "Feast of Music" venture, Sr. Geneviève wrote: "I am asking Saint Thérèse to help you, your secretary, and patrons of the Little Flower Hall in your beautiful work, and to obtain for you, your secretary and patrons the favours longed for, and sweetest gifts of Our Lady's Immaculate Heart."

The blessing seemed to work, as the twice-weekly recitals were soon packed to the gills. Fr. Hunt's initial idea was to gather just a few enthusiasts for a session. The first night exceeded expectations, with 29 turning up. Soon, numbers were topping the 100 mark. By 1955, the figure had grown to 129. "If the present rate of progress continues," a journalist wrote in October 1955, "he will have to look for larger premises to house the number of people whose appreciation of fine music he has done so much to foster."

Part of the attraction was that the hall felt like "a haven of pleasure," one patron reflected. Based in Dominick Street – appropriately named after Fr. Hunt's order, the Dominicans – it was ideally suited for the purpose intended. To sit in "the peaceful atmosphere of the Little Flower Hall" and to listen to the "rich music permeating the stillness" was sheer enjoyment, one attendee remarked. "When the lights are dimmed to a deep crimson or a pale blue, and the music comes forth, the audience is enveloped, as it were, in comfort," the enthusiast added.

Fr. Harry Hunt certainly made sure that his patrons were comfortable. An "air-conditioning motor" was installed in the hall's early days. Within two years, he had added 200 yards of curtain material to the premises, enveloping it from ceiling to floor. "I feared that the sound would have been interfered with," a patron commented on the new soft furnishings. "On the contrary it is better, if such were possible."

The priest also played a broad variety of recordings. They were chosen "to suit all tastes," a reviewer noted, adding that this helped to "increase one's knowledge of music." They would "bring oneself within the listen and learn orbit," he remarked. The amplification system helped, too, especially given that it was stereophonic – "the last word in amplification," the reviewer concluded.

The initial supply of records wasn't vast, by any means, with only 80 LPs in stock. High-quality recordings were expensive, retailing for almost £1 each. Fr. Hunt's plan was simple – pack the crowds in and the recordings would pay for themselves. By 1955, he was able to point to hundreds of pounds worth of stock, neatly filed in racks. "Limerick people will pay to hear good music," he explained, "and what they pay helps to build up our record library."

Above all, there was the sheer enthusiasm and dynamism of the man himself. Known to his numerous friends as "Father Harry" and to others as "The Smiling Dominican", he was actually a native of County Waterford. His father, who was manager and editor of *The Waterford News*, was an Englishman and a convert to Catholicism. Fr. Hunt described him as "a first-class

Catholic – a tip-top Catholic – and he and my mother certainly brought me up well."

Fr. Harry entered the Tallaght Novitiate in 1909, when he was almost 16. He moved to Rome in 1914 and three years later was ordained a Dominican. In his many later postings, he carried with him a love of music. This was no surprise as, at the age of 13, he could play the entire score of *Maritana* from memory. At the same age, he was earning two sovereigns for his performances over an entire week in Waterford's Theatre Royal. Later in life, he was known as an accomplished organist and as a piano player with a splendid keyboard technique.

It was no surprise, then, that Fr. Hunt became such a prominent figure in Limerick musical circles. Although popular, he was also a bit of a purist and took no prisoners in his quest for perfection. "How about having a cup of tea during the interval?" one regular suggested in the mid-1950s. "We come here not for a cup of tea but for the music," he replied.

He also wasted no time during the intervals, concentrating instead on the "Feast of Music". Yet his patrons loved him. As one person pointed out, even the flu wouldn't keep them away. "The Little Flower looks after her own, seemingly," that patron concluded.

Fr. Hunt additionally became known for his love of radio. "I travel the world on the short wave," he once said. He tuned into worldwide stations and corresponded with them over the years. It was not unknown to hear his name mentioned in broadcasts from the most obscure locations. It didn't matter if those locations adhered to Communism – so reviled at the time – arguing, just like Thérèse might, that love, and not hate, was all-important and "should be given a chance."

Fr. Harry Hunt died in 1978, at the age of 84. "He retained his cheerfulness and love of music to the end," one newspaper remarked, while also pointing out that he was "a general favourite wherever he ministered." But, in Limerick, it was for his "Feast of Music" sessions that he was most fondly recalled. His death brought back to mind a critic's comment in the *Limerick Leader* from 1958, some 20 years earlier.

"My congratulations and best wishes to Father Hunt on his great work of stirring up the smouldering fire of musical appreciation in our midst," the critic wrote. "I wholeheartedly recommend these recitals to all music lovers worthy of the name. Drop in some Monday night and I guarantee you'll come again. It's worth a trial, surely. You won't get a better shilling's worth."

A remarkable church dedicated to St. Thérèse of Lisieux was blessed and opened in Mount Merrion, Dublin, in 1956. It contains works by two noted Irish artists.

An Arctic cold spell paralysed Europe in late February 1956. Snowstorms and blizzards swept through the continent. Twenty-six people froze to death in West Germany. A child was killed, and many more injured, when a cinema roof collapsed near Rome. Storms lashed shipping in the English Channel, reducing visibility to zero. Road conditions in Britain were atrocious. "Never since the motor car became an integral part of the social fabric has road paralysis on this scale been experienced before," an A.A. spokesman said.

In Ireland, conditions were just as bad. Heavy snow fell in Dublin on Saturday, 18 February, causing the abandonment of many sporting fixtures, among them a Railway Cup football match at Croke Park. Campaigning in a by-election in North Kerry was all but abandoned following a deluge of icy cold rain. Snowdrifts covered the country, not least in the elevated Mount Merrion area of Dublin, where a new church was scheduled to open on Sunday, 19 February.

It was a big day in the modern history of Mount Merrion. Located four miles from central Dublin, it was once a place of green fields and market gardens. Urban sprawl had changed all that. By 1956, Mount Merrion's population had grown to almost 10,000, prompting commentators to refer to it as a "populous" suburb and noting that it had "grown up so rapidly in the housing drive." A new Catholic church was required to cater for the ever-expanding population.

St. Thérèse would have savoured the deathly-quiet, snow-covered day. She adored snow. "Its whiteness entranced me," she said in *Story of a Soul*, also reflecting that nothing matched the earth "clad in its beautiful white mantle." She liked snow so much that she hoped her clothing day – when she would receive her Carmelite habit – would be "decked, like myself, in spotless white."

Although her clothing day was set for early January, the weather was so mild it could have been spring. On emerging from the chapel, she saw – to her amazement – that, despite the mildness of the weather, the ground was covered with snow. "Since then, many people, hearing of my desire, have described this event as 'the little miracle' of my clothing day, and thought it strange I should be so fond of snow," she remarked.

We might wonder how many Mount Merrion residents, heading to their brand-new Church of St. Thérèse of Lisieux, would have recalled the Little Flower's love of snow. As they carefully made their way through the white landscape and along icy paths, dressed in their heavy overcoats and hats, the symbolic connection between the weather and the church must have crossed at least some people's minds. It certainly struck one of the assisting priests at the opening Mass – Fr. M. V. Rogers – who later remarked on how "fitting" the snow was.

The Archbishop of Dublin and Primate of Ireland, John Charles McQuaid, formally opened the new church. Having been presented with a golden key by the architect, Mr. J. J. Robinson, the door was unlocked, the church blessed, land deeds presented to the archbishop, and the first Mass celebrated in what was a truly impressive structure seating 1,800 people.

The new edifice, designed in a modern Renaissance style, continued the long tradition of church-building in Dublin, according to a report in *The Catholic Standard*. The weekly Catholic newspaper added that the structure was situated in a commanding location that "reveals the full beauty of its design" and was "eminently suitable in form and skyline to the fine site."

The highlight of the church was the side chapel of St. Thérèse, its patroness. The fresco in the shrine, representing the Little Flower, was painted by the artist Seán Keating. Not only was he one of the noted painters of his era, but he was also president of the Royal Hibernian Academy. A staunch Catholic, Keating was in his late 60s and had been going through a spell of painting many religious works. His depiction of St. Thérèse was described in the press as "striking" and one "which will rank with his best."

The Stations of the Cross were painted by another famous Irish artist, George Collie, who had been born in County Monaghan but lived in Dublin. A member of the Royal Hibernian Academy, he was chairman of the Arts Council for many years and ran his own art school in Dublin. His work for the Mount Merrion church was also acclaimed. It was described as "another outstanding contribution to Church art."

Both Collie and Keating were interviewed by the press in the week preceding the church opening. They were both touching up their respective works, indicating just how close their final preparations were to deadline day. The fundraising committee was hard at work, too. Given the high cost of the project, they were organising a concert at the Gresham Hotel for inauguration night in order to raise much-needed funds.

The overall project certainly had cost a tidy sum to complete. A multiplicity of fundraising schemes had been used to raise money, including fêtes, concerts and whist drives. The annual Mount Merrion fête became something of an event of the year. Despite these endeavours, the church was left with a debt of £86,000, which was substantial for the time. Later, a feature film about the birth of the new parish – and the building of the new church – was presented throughout Dublin, further defraying costs.

Every contribution helped; every donation had an impact; every gift played its role. It was like an enterprising project being fulfilled, an ambitious venture coming to fruition. But, then again, wasn't that what St. Thérèse had once said? From "under the snow" the "early spring flowers begin to come up," she had remarked in *Story of a Soul*. Perhaps that's what had been witnessed, on that cold, snow-covered day, at the church bearing her name in the Dublin suburb of Mount Merrion.

A song about St. Thérèse, sung by a Welshman of Irish heritage, was banned by the BBC in 1956 yet went on to enormous success in Ireland and Great Britain.

The saying "every cloud has a silver lining" is certainly appreciated in the music business, especially regarding records that are banned. The business is littered with discs that are barred from playlists yet go on to huge chart success. The publicity undoubtedly helps; the human frailty which insists that anything forbidden is worthwhile helps, too.

No one understood this better than the Welsh singer Malcolm Vaughan, whose mother was from Cork and whose recording *St. Thérèse of the Roses* was banned by the BBC. It immediately sold half a million records and jumped to No.3 in the charts, where it stayed for five months. The BBC had argued that the lyrics were "contrary both to Roman Catholic doctrine and to Protestant sentiment," as they put it. That the song was popular with the public didn't matter; it was banned, that was it!

The fact that the lyrics were utterly innocuous seemed of little concern to the BBC. Written by American composers Remus Harris and Arthur Strauss, the words spoke of a man's prayer said nightly to Thérèse asking her to bless his sweetheart and the love they shared, and to guide them and protect them in their years ahead as a married couple. It would be hard to find lyrics more innocent than that!

Released in October 1956, the recording was deemed worthy enough for BBC TV's *Off the Record* programme to invite Vaughan to appear on the show. The corporation had a quick change of heart after a committee decided that the song was unsuitable for broadcast, and the invitation was hastily withdrawn.

The press loved the story, revelling in the controversy. Radio Luxembourg loved it, too, doing everything it could to usurp its competitor and promote the disc. Record shops were the beneficiaries, selling bucket-loads of singles.

On the back of the record's success and his many other chart hits, Vaughan arrived in Ireland for a national tour in late 1958. Organised by Irish promoter Nelius O'Connell, he appeared at many venues including the National Ballroom in Dublin, Top Hat in Dun Laoghaire, Gaiety in Sligo, Showboat in Youghal and Olympia Ballroom in Waterford.

Everywhere he went he was recommended as a "must see", primarily for his rendition of *St. Thérèse of the Roses*. Playing to a packed house in Waterford, the local newspaper, *The Munster Express*, reported that he "won enthusiastic applause from patrons." They went on to say that he "gave delightful renderings of some of the numbers which have made his name famous" throughout Britain and Ireland, among them *More than Ever* – which was doing well in the charts – and others including, of course, his song about St. Thérèse.

Some critics were effusive in their praise, with the *Evening Herald* being particularly enthusiastic: "Malcolm Vaughan – praises be – is not a rocker or a roller. What he does is the time-honoured old routine. It pulled them in in Cleopatra's time and it'll be pulling them in when Presley's Christian (?) name will be thought of – if anybody has the time to think of it at all – as a printer's error." Although it was only two years earlier, in 1956, that Presley had his first No.1 pop success with *Heartbreak Hotel*, the critic's remark was unfortunate, to say the least!

Another reviewer, writing in *The Sligo Champion*, said: "Malcolm Vaughan cannot be compared with most pop singers of today. His is a rich, lyrical voice with feeling, with range and perfect sincerity." On the other hand, the *Limerick Leader* was particularly devastating when referring to his rendition of *The Holy City*. "About this the only adequate comment I can make is 'Jerusalem'! Here we have the definite recording of the ballad; that is, if you want to be absolutely sure how not to sing it...I am sure that anybody who knows anything at all about music will writhe in horror."

We are not sure if the audience at Vaughan's show in Sligo were "writhing in horror" over his singing or, indeed, incensed, like the BBC, by the lyrics of *St. Thérèse of the Roses*. Whatever the cause, mayhem ensued. A front-page headline in *The Sligo Champion* summed it up: "Disorderly Scenes outside Cinema after 'Pop' Singer's Show." Not only was Vaughan's Volkswagen Microbus damaged – its tyres deflated and rear-view mirror broken – but a riot erupted on the street. Garda reinforcements had to be called and batons were drawn.

Even though seven men and a girl were bound over to keep the peace for two years – and fined sums ranging from £1 to £3 – the episode was grist to the mill for Vaughan. He had seen controversy before with *St. Thérèse of the Roses*; the fact that it had surfaced again was good for business. The tour was a sell-out and his records sold well as a result.

The name of St. Thérèse also remained in the headlines for many months, thanks to Vaughan. In fact, it could be said that no one did more to popularise the saint in Ireland and Britain in the latter years of the 1950s than the Welsh star. While he failed to replicate that success in America, another version of the song, by Billy Ward and his Dominoes, reached No.27 on the *Billboard* Hot 100, securing even more fame for the Little Flower among transatlantic audiences.

Malcolm Vaughan continued to perform in the pop music business for many years, before eventually retiring to his home in Eastbourne, England, where he died on 9 February 2010. He had, by then, chalked up eight Top 20 hits, including a recording of the theme song, *A Night to Remember*, from the 1958 film about the sinking of the *Titanic*. However, it is for something else that he will be long remembered – as a singer who, according to *The Sligo Champion* in 1958, "rocketed to stardom a little over 12 months ago with the famous recording *St. Thérèse of the Roses*."

Dorothy Day, the American champion of the poor and a convert to Catholicism, had great belief in Thérèse of Lisicux. Not only did she write a book on the saint in 1960, but she is currently a candidate for canonisation.

The first time Dorothy Day heard of St. Thérèse she was lying in the maternity ward of Bellevue Hospital, New York. The year was 1926. Her bed was next to a window overlooking the East River, where tiny tugboats and long tankers floated by. Each morning, the sun cast its light on the water outside. When the fog rolled in, the view disappeared. On those occasions, "the sound of fog horns haunted the day and the night," she recalled.

Around that time, Day was working for the Anti-Imperialist League, a Communist Party affiliate with offices in Union Square, Manhattan. She had an interesting family history, with strong Irish roots. One of her grandfathers was a doctor and had volunteered for the Confederate army during the Civil War. Her father, John Day, was a journalist who, for a time, wrote a column for the New York *Morning Telegraph*.

Driven by what Pope Francis would later refer to as her "passion for justice," she became a journalist, activist, pacifist and champion of the poor. In her early years, she wrote for several socialist and progressive publications in America. Among the notables she interviewed was Leon Trotsky, the Marxist revolutionary and Soviet politician who was assassinated in 1940. She also agitated for the right of women to vote.

Day eventually became a devout Catholic, co-founding *The Catholic Worker*, a newspaper promoting Church teachings on social issues. The publication was part of the Catholic Worker Movement, which had similar aims. Her work included the establishment of homes for people in need. Ultimately, Day became a candidate for canonisation. But that was in the future. First, there was that 60-bed ward in Bellevue Hospital where, as a radical with no particular religious affiliation, she gave birth to her tiny child.

"What are you going to name your baby?" the woman in the next bed asked Dorothy. "Tamar Teresa," she replied, explaining that her friend's little girl was named Tamar, meaning little palm tree in Hebrew. "And Teresa is after the Little Flower?" the woman queried. Dorothy was stumped. She had never heard of the Little Flower, although she had heard of St. Teresa of Ávila, whose vigorous writing and sense of humour had inspired the choice of her baby's name.

The woman, who was a Catholic, reached in her handbag, rooted through her powder and lipstick, her money, tissues and rosary beads, and produced a medal of the Little Flower. "Here,

I will give it to you for your baby," she said. "Pin it on her."
Although fearing that the baby might swallow it, or that the pin
might come loose, Dorothy took the medal. Two saints, she
thought, were better than one!

The next time Dorothy Day heard of St. Thérèse of Lisieux
was in 1928, a year before Wall Street collapsed and the Great
Depression began. At that stage, she was 30 years old. Before
that, in 1927, she had been baptised a Catholic. Although she
had read the Bible, along with the works of St. Augustine and
The Imitation of Christ by Thomas à Kempis, she was clueless
about modern-day saints.

All that changed when an Augustinian priest gave her a book
to read. It was *Story of a Soul*, by St. Thérèse of Lisieux. She
wasn't impressed. The writing seemed to Dorothy to be "like
that of a schoolgirl." Having read it, her reaction was even
more caustic. "I found it colourless, monotonous, too small in
fact for my notice....Joan of Arc leading an army fitted more
into my concept of a saint," she remarked.

Dorothy soon changed her tune and became smitten by the
saint. Not only did she study *Story of a Soul* but she also read
the Little Flower's poetry and *Novissima Verba* (her last words,
transcribed by her sister Pauline). She decided to write a book
about Thérèse, which she worked on for more than five years.
Despite being rejected by her publisher, the book eventually hit
the shelves in 1960. It turned out to be a brilliant evocation and
analysis of the saint's life.

In her book, Day explained how Thérèse's little way was "an
explosive force" capable of transforming lives. "It has all the
power of the spirit of Christianity behind it," she wrote. It was
a philosophy that appealed to the masses – the common men

and women who had spread her fame by word of mouth and proclaimed her a saint. These were the Catholics, young and old, married and single, who felt hopeless and useless, less than the dust, ineffectual, wasted and powerless. "To a great extent she has made her appeal to all of these," Day reflected.

And how did Thérèse accomplish this? Essentially, she was holy – "she was just good, good as the bread which the Normans bake in huge loaves," Day wrote. "She practised the presence of God and she did all things – all the little things that make up our daily life and contact with others – for his honour and glory. She did not need much time to expound what she herself called 'her little way,' which she said was for all. She wrote her story, and God did the rest."

Following its publication, Dorothy's book, *Thérèse*, became something of a classic. One reviewer remarked that it "captures the heart of the message of Saint Thérèse of Lisieux" while also revealing "the depth of Dorothy's own spirituality." Another reviewer referred to it as a vital legacy "for anyone whose life is dedicated to working for peace and justice."

The pursuit of those two ideals – peace and justice – remained the hallmark of Dorothy Day's life right up to the time of her death in 1980. To Dorothy, they weren't just abstract concepts or fanciful notions; instead, they were principles she applied in her everyday life. She didn't only write about the poor – she fed them and lived a life not unlike theirs. She was also willing to be imprisoned for her convictions.

That sense of purity and holiness led, in 2000, to Cardinal John O'Connor, Archbishop of New York, formally requesting the Congregation for the Causes of Saints to consider her as a candidate for canonisation. Although the process is still far from complete, in many ways it hardly matters. As she once pointed out, it is not just canonised saints that are beloved by God. "So are we all," she said – an assertion that certainly applies in the case of Dorothy Day.

The Earl of Wicklow rekindled interest in St. Thérèse in the early 1960s. He did so through a book he translated and published in 1961.

The first comprehensive study of the life and death of Azélie Martin – mother of St. Thérèse – was brought to the Irish public in book form in 1961. Although Thérèse had written about her mother in *Story of a Soul*, there had been no detailed English language publication on this formidable woman up to the turn of the 1960s. All that changed thanks to the Earl of Wicklow.

The Earl had an extraordinary life. To begin with, the name he was given at birth, in 1902, was memorable, to say the least. William Cecil James Philip John Paul Howard – as he was called – was born into the Anglo-Irish aristocracy and was educated at Eton and Oxford University. He fitted in, especially given his illustrious background, which was filled with earls, dukes, lords and ladies.

It was inevitable, during his years at school, that William would be assigned a manageable schoolboy-friendly nickname. To many, he became known simply as "Billy Wicklow". He was also called "Cracky" Clonmore – a reference to both his effervescent, happy-go-lucky air and his early title, Lord Clonmore. Among his fellow students was the author Evelyn Waugh, who became not only a friend but inveigled him into the famous "Brideshead set".

Although initially an Anglican, Billy converted to Catholicism in 1932, when he was 30 years of age. His conversion caused mayhem within his family. His father – Ralph Howard, the seventh Earl of Wicklow – disinherited him. He was also told to steer clear of his family home in Ireland on Sundays because of his habit of attending Mass in the company of housemaids and general domestic help.

Nothing deterred Billy, and after 1946, when he took over from his father as Earl of Wicklow, he embarked on some remarkable religious ventures. Not only did he write books of a Catholic nature – including one on Pope Pius XI and another on the Irish monk, Dom Marmion – but he also became well known as a Catholic publisher. The company he ran – Clonmore & Reynolds – developed into one of the most reputable Irish publishers of its day.

It was around this time that St. Thérèse worked her way into his life. She did so through a biography of her mother, Azélie Martin, who had shaped the saint's early years. The book, which had originally been published in 1951, was titled *Azélie Martin: Mère de Sainte Thérèse de l'Enfant-Jésus*, by Louise André-Delastre. Billy decided it was time to bring his proficiency at French into action, and he set about translating the text.

The hardback version of the book – titled *Azélie Martin: Mother of the Little Flower* – found its way onto Irish bookshop shelves in late 1961. Published by Clonmore & Reynolds, it received mostly good, although not unanimously favourable, reviews. *The Drogheda Independent* praised it for providing "an authentic picture of a woman of courage, resource and initiative," adding that the publication was "an illuminating picture of an unforgettable personality."

The Connacht Sentinel agreed, saying "this biography gives a vivid picture of the life of a great woman. As the mother of nine children and for a long time the bread winner, it shows a woman who had courage, endurance and great faith." Unfortunately, the *Irish Independent* took a contrary view, slamming the book for "its complete lack of literary merit" and for being "utterly devoid of style and at times disjointed," although it did concede that the work presented "a lively and sympathetic picture of the mother of the Little Flower."

Whatever about arguments over its merits and demerits, the book certainly provided a comprehensive overview of Azélie's life. It particularly described, in detail, the suffering and sorrow surrounding her death. Struck down by breast cancer, she battled bravely with the disease in the short time that remained of her life. "You who created me, have pity on me," she sometimes cried out in utter distress, according to the book. Eventually, on Tuesday, 28 August 1877, she died.

"Billy Wicklow" or "Cracky" Clonmore, as he was once called, died just over 100 years after Azélie, in 1978. His passing, at the age of 75, was noted in the national press. He warranted an editorial in one newspaper – *The Irish Press* – which referred to him as "a good and cultured Irishman." The editorial also referred to his work as "a distinguished Catholic layman, publisher and activist on behalf of St. Vincent de Paul and many other charitable organisations."

With his death, his title – Earl of Wicklow – passed to his first cousin. It did so because Billy had no children. Eventually, when the cousin died, the title became extinct. The book on Azélie Martin also faded from view and, today, is almost impossible to find. Just like Billy, the book has become a footnote to history, with the odd faded copy reminding us of a time when he turned his mind to the enduring legacy of Azélie Martin, the mother of a saint.

The distinguished Irish-American preacher and broadcaster, Archbishop Fulton Sheen, was an admirer of Thérèse, as he recalled during a series of lectures he gave in Dublin, in 1973.

Archbishop Fulton Sheen recalled an insightful event concerning the young Thérèse in a sermon delivered in Dublin. The incident involved Sr. St. Pierre, one of the older nuns in the Carmel. Sick and infirm, she was notoriously cantankerous and difficult to deal with. She needed assistance as she was arthritic and barely able to shuffle from her cell.

Thérèse offered to act as her helper. She knew what she was getting into, saying: "It cost me a lot to offer myself for this little service because I knew it wasn't easy to please this poor sister." How right she was! When helping the nun to walk, not only did she have to hold the ageing sister's belt in a particular way but, if she took a misstep, Thérèse would be blamed for holding the belt incorrectly.

Among her jobs was to help Sr. St. Pierre from the choir to the refectory. "She had to be aided as she walked, had to sit down in a chair in a special way, and had to have the bread broken for her in the bowl, always in a special way, for she had done it that way for 50 years," Archbishop Sheen noted in his sermon.

No matter what Thérèse did, or how hard she tried, Sr. St. Pierre railed at her, saying she was too young, didn't know how to do anything, and was obviously trying to kill her. "I can't feel your hand anymore, you let go of me, I'm going to fall," was a common refrain. Similar remarks had prompted other sisters to run a mile. In contrast, Thérèse would just smile.

One day, while she was helping Sr. St. Pierre to the refectory, Thérèse heard music from afar. Her mind drifted, and before her eyes she imagined a great ballroom, with people dancing, music playing and plenty of chatter. A sense of joy overwhelmed her. Suddenly returning to reality, she looked down at the elderly nun. She said aloud that even for all the happiness and joyful music in the world she would never trade her Sr. St. Pierre.

Thérèse's kindness and consideration didn't go unnoticed. The young novice was soon in the ageing nun's good graces. Later, Sr. St. Pierre spoke to a new arrival at the Carmel, saying she had "something very important" to tell her. The information concerned the acts of goodness Thérèse had been practising on her behalf. "That child will go far," she said, clearly appreciating the importance of Thérèse's little way.

Fulton Sheen, the great Irish-American theologian, preacher and broadcaster – whose maternal roots were in Croghan, County Roscommon and whose father was of Irish descent – also grasped the message of the Little Flower. The message, he said, was straightforward – Thérèse wanted everything to be simple. Even her description of how we could become saints, he said, was the same – simple.

Her philosophy reminded him of a conversation he once had with Pope John XXIII, where the pope had said: "I always try to avoid the complicated things of life. I want everything to be simple." Thérèse's message was just like the pope's – all things are simple, everything matters, especially the sacrifices we make in life. "Love lives only by sacrifice," she had remarked. No one could have missed how she applied that thinking in the case of Sr. St. Pierre.

Archbishop Sheen's sermons went down a treat in Dublin, but that was no surprise. After all, he was already famous as a radio preacher in America, where his *Catholic Hour* broadcasts had reached four million people every Sunday afternoon. His television audiences for his *Life is Worth Living* broadcasts had amounted to some 30 million viewers each show.

He was also a theologian of note, having graduated from St. Paul Seminary in Minnesota, Catholic University in Washington D.C. and the University of Louvain in Belgium. His preaching was equally remarkable, as was evident from his sermons delivered at the Carmelite Church, Whitefriar Street, Dublin.

As one letter writer to *The Irish Press* remarked of his talks: "That so many people, including priests and nuns, were so greatly taken by the eloquence and personal holiness of Archbishop Sheen, is beyond doubt.... By means of his concrete images, together with his constant aim to proclaim the primacy of the spiritual over the material, he succeeds in winning minds and – I have no doubt – hearts."

In his sermons, Archbishop Sheen certainly caught both the "mind" and "heart" of St. Thérèse. Compiled later on in an insightful book – *Archbishop Fulton Sheen's St. Thérèse: A Treasured Love Story* – the sermons captured numerous facets of her life, including her virtues, fortitude, humility, charity, love of prayer, and her total grasp of the Old and New Testaments. Most importantly, they highlighted her kindness and compassion.

Those self-denying, benevolent features of her personality, according to Archbishop Sheen, are relevant to how we care for people today. "Think of how many circumstances we all have in life where we have to take care of people," he said. In every sickness, we can offer up our sufferings. "I think the hand of Christ is in the 'glove' of every sick person, and all we ever see is the glove. But inside is the hand of Christ who gave us that suffering."

How we should deal with suffering, and become a saint, is readily apparent in the story of Sr. St. Pierre. It's a very "modern" philosophy, Archbishop Sheen concluded. "There is no need of anyone wearing a hair shirt," he said. That's in the past. Our neighbours are hair shirts. Life is a hair shirt. "Your housework, your office work, whatever you happen to do, that's where you start." That's where you need to practise kindness and consideration. That's where you begin to become a saint, he concluded.

There is a remarkable Irish story connected to St. Thérèse's elevation to the status of Doctor of the Church. The story comes from County Cork.

On 19 October 1997, St. Thérèse was made a Doctor of the Church. The accolade is a prestigious one, reserved for saints of "outstanding holiness" whose writings are deemed of particular note. She became only the third woman to receive the title – the others being St. Catherine of Siena and St. Teresa of Ávila. Having died aged 24, Thérèse was the youngest saint in history – and only the thirty-third in all – to be so honoured.

The event, held in Rome, was spectacular. Pope John Paul II concelebrated Mass in St. Peter's Square with 16 cardinals, bishops and priests. Next to the altar was a metal urn containing relics of the saint. It was a poignant reminder of that day, more than a century earlier, when Thérèse had arrived in Rome as a 14-year-old to ask for the pope's help to become a nun.

Pope John Paul II delivered the homily, saying that Thérèse's "spiritual path is so mature and ardent, the intuitions of faith present in her writings are so vast and profound, as to have earned her a place among the great masters of the spirit." Her "little path," he added, "leads to the secret of every existence" and enlightens "the mind and heart of those who are thirsting for truth and love."

Back in Ireland, there was one man who had every reason to smile at the events taking place that day. His name is Eamonn Moynihan, from Banteer, County Cork. A year earlier, the importance of that particular date – 19 October 1997 – had been revealed to him in the strangest of ways. The story is a remarkable one and worth recalling.

Eamonn inherited a love for Thérèse from his mother, Mary, who died in 2005. A long time before that, in the early 1930s, she had become a devotee of the saint. "I developed my devotion as a result of my mother," Eamonn said. "We used to get a calendar every year and St. Thérèse's picture would be on it. It attracted me to her. We did novenas and I always prayed to her. Eventually, I called her 'my guiding star'."

In time, Eamonn organised prayer meetings in the school hall in his town. "It would hold about 100," he recalled, "and I brought in all kinds of speakers. I did them from 1985 – 1996. I then switched to the community centre." Having decided on the new venue, which was larger, he set about organising an appropriate event. It was now September 1996, more than a year before Thérèse's event in Rome, and 11 months before it was announced.

"I wanted to have a big day of prayer and I wondered what day to hold it on," Eamonn recollects. "One day, I was looking at a picture of St. Thérèse and she seemed to speak to me. It wasn't actually a loud voice. It's hard to describe. It was like it was coming up from my heart into my head, probably more like a revelation.

"She said, 'Have a big day in the hall and crowds will come.' She said to book the hall and arrange it for 19 October 1997. I hadn't a clue why that date was singled out. It was also more than a year away. I then said, 'Where will I get a priest?' She named Fr. Ryan, the Carmelite, from Kildare, who had been organising events for St. Thérèse. She said to contact him and he would give the talk and say the prayers.

"I booked the hall and contacted the priest. He said, 'I'm an old man now, and I wouldn't be able to travel down.' He then told me, 'There's another man, Fr. Eugene McCaffrey. He's your man.' So he gave me his number and he answered the phone straightaway. I told him I wanted him to come down a year away, on 19 October 1997. He looked at his diary and said, 'No problem. I'll come.'

"Christmas passed by, and so did spring. That summer, I got a phone call from the priest. It was around August. He said, 'Do you realise what you are after doing?' I asked him what he meant. He then asked me how I knew. I wondered what he was trying to get at. He told me, 'The pope has just made 19 October the day when St. Thérèse will become a Doctor of the Church!'

"The priest was puzzled and amazed. I told him the story of how it was St. Thérèse who had told me what to do. He found it extraordinary. He said he had been asked to go to Rome for the ceremony, but he was going to come to us instead. He did come, and the place was packed. People came from everywhere. There were 12 fifty-seat buses there. They came from Cork, Thurles, Limerick, Clare, Waterford, West Cork, Listowel, Tralee – they came from all over. It was a huge success."

For the record, research bears out the dates in the story you have read. "Nothing puzzles me," Eamonn concludes. "The strangest things can happen. God is everywhere. And I think St. Thérèse is wonderful, a beautiful saint. She was so simple, so loving. The idea that you should do simple little things for Jesus was really great. She speaks to anyone who listens and who trusts in God. I believe she spoke to me that day, no doubt."

Relics of St. Thérèse arrived in Ireland on 15 April 2001. Scenes of euphoria were witnessed as the relics travelled the country up to their departure on 2 July.

More than 1,000 people stood in wait at the harbour in Rosslare, County Wexford, to welcome the arrival of Thérèse's relics to Irish shores. A reverential silence descended on the crowd as the reliquary, weighing 400 pounds, was carried ashore by six military pallbearers. An army guard of honour and garda escort lined the route for the transfer of the saint's remains from the harbour to St. Patrick's Church in Rosslare.

Although those in attendance noted the solemnity of the occasion, few anticipated the national outburst of devotion that would follow in the months ahead. Encouraged no doubt by the fine weather, between two and three million people, including the young, old, sick and healthy, packed themselves into churches or lined the streets to pay their respects to the saint. Not since the arrival of President John F. Kennedy in 1963 had the nation witnessed anything like it.

The turnout was extraordinary. A mile-long line of people queued at Beaumont church, Dublin, to see the relics. Sixty thousand waited for up to three hours at St. John's Cathedral, Limerick. Forty thousand people crammed into the Carmelite monastery in Tallow, County Waterford – a number that would have shocked the five Carmelite sisters who, in 1836, founded the monastery after travelling by Bianconi coach from Dublin.

Some who viewed the relics were driven by a burning conviction; others came out of mild curiosity; more felt drawn to a unique national event. The demand was so great, the queues so long, the fervour so intense that churches were forced to keep their doors open through the night. Businesses put up their shutters. Houses were festooned with flags and bunting. Traffic ground to a halt. "We knew it was going to be big but it exceeded our most optimistic expectations," Fr. Linus Ryan, the visit coordinator, remarked.

Flower sellers did brisk business. "People are buying mostly red roses, because in St. Thérèse's picture there are red roses all around her," one vendor told the *Irish Examiner*. There were blue roses, too, with the seller proclaiming: "Buy a blue one for Our Lady." An enterprising Galway trader explained: "We're all the one family, uncles, nephews, nieces. And we've been to all the centres – to Ennis, Galway, Tuam, Loughrea – everywhere the relics have been, we've sold our roses."

The relics, stored in a gilt-edged casket and enclosed in a perspex dome, were transported by Thérèsemobile through the country. The vehicle carrying the intricately-carved wooden reliquary was driven by former army man Pat Sweeney, who had served in all ranks of the defence forces right up to sergeant major. "I am very pleased to be part of it," said Pat, who was not only an admirer of the Little Flower but had visited the Carmel in Lisieux on several occasions. He had a daughter and granddaughter named after Thérèse.

Among the locations the Thérèsemobile visited were the prisons at Mountjoy and Limerick. Both stopovers were a great success. No doubt, the saint would have been pleased, especially given that, as a young teenager, she had prayed for a French murderer by the name of Pranzini. Worried that he might be executed without repenting, she prayed to God for a sign that he would be saved. She later read in a newspaper that, as Pranzini mounted the scaffold, he took hold of a priest's crucifix and kissed it three times. This, she believed, was her sign.

Further signs appeared in the summer of 2001, this time of miracles reported in the national press. One County Louth woman described how her chronic arthritis was cured following a visit to Thérèse's relics. Barely able to leave her home, she had to be lifted into her husband's car to make the trip. By the next morning, an improvement was noticeable. Soon, she was fully mobile. "I can move every part of my body for the first time since 1964 and this has been the way since the very first night I saw the relics," she said.

Another woman, from County Mayo, explained that for the first seven years of their marriage she and her husband had been childless. Having prayed to the Little Flower, they conceived their first child. They called her Teresa. A third woman, from County Cork, outlined how her sister, who was seriously ill, recovered her health after being given a rose-shaped medal of Thérèse, which had come all the way from Alençon.

Yet another woman, once again a County Cork resident, recounted how her grandchild had been saved from a burning house thanks to the Little Flower. The two-year-old had been in her room when fire broke out. A vase containing a rose which had touched Thérèse's casket was also in the room. The child's mother and a neighbour battled their way through smoke to rescue her. They found the child huddled in a corner and surrounded by petals from the rose, laid out in a circle. "This was a miracle," the grandmother concluded. "I think differently of St. Thérèse now."

Having travelled the length and breadth of Ireland, the relics of St. Thérèse finally left the country on 2 July 2001. They departed just as the mini-heatwave of the previous week was coming to a close. The bright sunshine seemed to be something of a metaphor for the visit, which had extended over 11 weeks and seen outpourings of religious fervour not witnessed since the arrival of Pope John Paul II in 1979 or, before that, the Eucharistic Congress in 1932.

Thérèse departed just as she had arrived back in April. Her casket was carried aboard a ferry at Rosslare by the same military unit that had brought her ashore. Crowds gave her a joyous send-off. The Little Flower then began her journey back to Cherbourg and, from there, to Lisieux. "It has been a very long few months," Fr. Linus Ryan, the visit coordinator, reflected. "We are a little bit frayed at the edges, but it is not every day you have the privilege of carrying the remains of a saint around your country. It was a once in a lifetime opportunity."

Carmel, from the midlands, describes how her son was cured following a visit to the relics of St. Thérèse.

In 2001, Carmel's baby boy wasn't hearing properly. He was screaming a lot – a high-pitched scream – and his head seemed squashed. Later on, his speech development was clearly delayed. Carmel was worried. "I had brought him to see many specialists, who told me there was nothing wrong, but I had a feeling there was," she said. "I knew he was far from fine."

Time passed by and still the problem persisted. The medical advice didn't change. "He'll be fine," she was repeatedly told. She knew they were wrong. "I was at the end of the road," she now recalls. "When you don't know what's wrong with your child, and everybody is telling you something different, you become terrified and fearful. It's a horrible place to be."

At that stage, Carmel didn't pray to St. Thérèse, although her mother had great devotion. Things changed, however, when the Little Flower's relics came to a nearby town. Having decided to travel to see them, she and her husband Hugh set off by car with their son.

"There were queues and queues of people outside," Carmel recalled of the scene confronting them when they arrived at the church. "Our son was very agitated, really screeching. It all seemed hopeless. However, instead of going home, I decided to go around to the back of the church and a priest saw me. He gave me a prayer card and brought me and my child in to see the relics. We didn't get close to them. I had hoped for a miracle and that he would be cured instantly, but it didn't happen. We just went in and came out again. Then we left for home.

"When we were driving home, initially I felt it was all a waste of time. Then the strangest thing happened. I suddenly had an image of my son being cut from ear to ear, right across his head. I saw it as clear as day. It was very strange. The image meant nothing to me; no one had mentioned surgery or anything like that. I don't know where it came from and I didn't know what it meant, although I did say it to my husband, who was beside me in the car.

"From then on, I started to pray with the little prayer card. I prayed to Thérèse like I had never prayed before. I felt like I was begging. When you have a child who is sick, you will try anything. I didn't have anything else. I knew how much Thérèse had suffered. I also knew how her parents had suffered, having lost four children. I kept asking her: 'Please get us through this. Please help us.'"

There was no immediate cure for Carmel's son, no sense that her child might ever be well again. Eventually, however, she and her husband decided to bring him to a surgeon. "I was desperate at this stage," Carmel recalls. "He was getting worse and starting to lose his sight, his balance, his speech. When we got him to the hospital, the surgeon examined him and he then sat us down.

"He told us that when our son was born the bones didn't meet properly at the top of his head. He said he had nerve damage in both ears. His hearing was affected; so was his speech. It was hard to believe but he drew us a circle on the page and explained: 'We will have to cut him from ear to ear.' It was exactly the same as the image I had seen in the car. And that's what they did.

"They did the operation, cut him from ear to ear, plated his head and remoulded it back together again. They did a great job, and we brought him home. It was probably the toughest time of our lives. The medical people wrote off every bit of hope we had – they have to do that, I suppose. He also ended up being strapped in for six months and he couldn't sleep in his cot. There were other tough times ahead.

"Eventually, he started school and ended up doing well. He totally turned a corner, academically and otherwise. He got involved in football and all the rest of it. Everything was back – his hearing, his speech, the lot. Having been told he would never talk, it had all changed. He became the nicest lad you would ever come across. It was all thanks to the operation.

"If we hadn't gone for that operation, in another six months it would have been too late. I believe Thérèse interceded that time we went to see her relics. I was at the end of the road. I had prayed all that time to her. I still do so now. I also have that prayer card to this day. It's dirty now and covered with tape. But I will never forget the day I got it – the day we went to see the relics, back in 2001. I didn't want to go there, but I felt I had to go. That was the day I trace our miracle back to."

Pope Francis, who once spent three months in Ireland, is a long-time devotee of St. Thérèse. This story begins when he was a cardinal in Argentina.

The night of 6 August 2010 was the worst possible time for the future Pope Francis to become ill. All that night, he lay awake in his bed suffering from an agonising pain in his leg. Medication was having no effect. The following morning, 7 August, he looked dreadful. Matters weren't helped by the weather, which was icy and wet. His press secretary, Federico Wals, was appalled by the state he was in.

Both Wals and Cardinal Bergoglio – as Pope Francis was called then – had good reason to be worried about the day ahead. It was the feast day of St. Cajetan, one of Argentina's most popular saints. It was Bergoglio's duty to celebrate Mass at the saint's shrine in Buenos Aires. He was also expected to walk past a mile-long line of pilgrims and greet them, as he had done in years gone by.

Although the gruelling task looked beyond him, Bergoglio explained to his press secretary that he had prayed to St. Thérèse and, God willing, things would work out. He limped along the first block of people, shaking hands and extending greetings. Wals noted that the cardinal's features were wracked with pain and felt he could walk no further. He was not surprised when, at the start of the second block, Bergoglio asked that his car should await him at the next corner.

Suddenly, out of nowhere, a tall, heavyset, middle-aged man appeared. Withdrawing his arm from inside his coat, he produced a white rose which he gave to Bergoglio. The cardinal took it, stared at the man and blessed him, without saying a word. By this stage, Wals and Bergoglio were near the car. Wals began to usher the cardinal towards it, but was instantly rebuffed. "This is the message I've been waiting for," the future pope said. "It will be okay now. This is the presence of Santa Teresita....We're going to make it." He walked the full ten blocks after that, and had no further pain in his leg.

Long before he became a cardinal, Jorge Mario Bergoglio was a devotee of St. Thérèse. He was an early practitioner of a novena to the Little Flower devised by a fellow Jesuit, Fr. Putigan.

Seeking a favour, Fr. Putigan began the famous novena in 1925. It involved the recitation, over nine days, of 24 Glory be to the Fathers. The number 24 represented how many years Thérèse had spent on earth.

There was an additional twist to the novena, which must have interested Bergoglio. Anxious to know that his novena was being heard, Fr. Putigan asked St. Thérèse to send him a sign in the form of a rose. On the novena's third day, that's exactly what happened – an unknown person handed him a beautiful rose. Later that year, during the second recitation of the novena, he made the same request. On the fourth day, he was again handed a rose, this time by a nurse who said, "St. Thérèse sent you this."

Bergoglio also read *Story of a Soul*. It appealed to his innate sense of humility and simplicity. In keeping with her message, he chose not to live in the archbishop's palace in Buenos Aires but in an apartment where he cooked for himself. He also frequently travelled by bus. A photograph of Thérèse was prominently positioned in his library, with a vase of white roses in front of it. When he sent letters, he would make sure to enclose her picture.

In 1980, having recently completed his time as provincial superior of the Jesuits in Argentina, Bergoglio spent three months in Dublin. During his sabbatical, he stayed at the Jesuit Centre in the Milltown Institute, where he studied English and also recovered from the trying times he had experienced under Argentina's military junta. He walked around Dublin 6 – through the grounds of Gonzaga College and Milltown Park – while living the sort of life of simplicity and contemplation he had learnt from St. Thérèse.

His devotion continued during his time as a cardinal and pope in Rome. As a cardinal, he would pray at a statue of Thérèse in a little Franciscan church in the Borgo, close to the Vatican. As pope, he practised the simplicity and austerity of her little way, living in a suite in the Casa Santa Marta, the Vatican City's guesthouse. He chose to travel in a modest car, sitting up front beside the driver, foregoing the traditional chauffeur-driven transport. He also notably confessed to falling asleep while praying. "St. Thérèse of the Child Jesus did that, too," he said by way of exoneration!

A close scrutiny of his speeches and sermons reveals just how closely he follows her little way. "The true greatness of man consists in making himself small before God," he once said as pope, adding that God is not known through "grand ideas and extensive study, but rather through the littleness of a humble and trusting heart. To be great before the Most High does not require the accumulation of honour and prestige or earthly goods and success, but rather a complete self-emptying."

On another occasion, he said: "St. Thérèse of Lisieux invites us to practise the little way of love, not to miss out on a kind word, a smile or any small gesture which sows peace and friendship." He added, on a further occasion, that to practise her little way to God, we need to have the trust of a little child who falls asleep without fear in his father's arms. "Jesus does not demand great actions from us, but simply surrender and gratitude," he remarked.

Above all, he spoke of her "roses" – those messages from Thérèse that guide his way. "When I have a problem, I ask the saint not to solve it but to take it in her hands and help me accept it. And as a sign, I almost always receive a white rose," he said. Whether handed to him by a nun, gardener or stranger off the street, to Pope Francis they are the signs, signals – even proofs – that Thérèse is listening, that she has heard his appeal, and that God is responding to his servant on earth and answering his prayers.

A chance meeting in Lourdes between two Irish people and two Americans brought to light an extraordinary story of an apparition involving St. Thérèse. The meeting took place in the early 2010s.

The High Stations of the Cross are a well-known landmark in Lourdes. Set on a steep, wooded hill, the 15 stations retrace Christ's sufferings along a beautiful rustic path. It was here, at the last three stations, that two County Cork pilgrims – Nora and Imelda – found themselves in the company of two other English-speaking visitors. Introductions were made, conversation ensued, and soon the two women were being enthralled by one man's personal experience of an apparition involving St. Thérèse.

"At the last three stations, there were these two gentlemen from America, who looked like two priests," Nora explained. "We stayed with them and prayed with them. It turned out that one of them was a missionary priest; the other was his friend. I happened to mention that I had a first-class relic of St. Thérèse with me. The friend said, 'Oh, my God! I don't believe it. We're going to Lisieux tomorrow.'

"He then turned to the priest and said, 'Tell them your story.' The priest said, 'It would take too long.' I said, 'Well, I have all day. How long have you got?' He started laughing and proceeded to tell his story. He said that he was once very sick – at one stage, dying – and that he had a steel rod inserted to keep his back upright. When he was having that operation, he nearly died a few times. He wasn't able to drink or eat.

"One day, in the hospital, a little nurse came to him and said, 'What did you drink today?' He said, 'Nothing, you know I can't keep it down.' She said, 'I'll go out and get you something and you can sip it very slowly.' She eventually came back with a drink, which looked like cranberry juice. He sipped it and found he could keep it down.

"The nurse attended him for all the time he was in hospital. His sister came to visit him; so did her son, his nephew. One day, the nurse said to the sister, 'You are very worried your brother is going to die.' She said she was. The nurse said, 'He'll be alright.' She gave the sister some prayer cards, which she put in her pocket. She thought no more of them.

"Eventually, the priest recovered and went back to his sister's house in Manhattan to recover. When he got better, he returned with his sister to the hospital to find the nurse and say thanks. He made enquiries about where she was, but there was no sign of her. He had a name but they said they never had a nurse with that name. He described her but they said they couldn't recognise the description. They went through their files and ended up saying there was nothing more they could do.

"The priest and his sister went back home. They were talking about how strange it all was. Eventually, the nephew arrived home and, after he heard what had happened, said, 'That's strange, because I met her, too.' Then the sister remembered the prayer cards. She found them. As she was going through them, the nephew looked at one and said, 'But that was her!' It was a picture of St. Thérèse!"

There is nothing new in apparitions like this being reported concerning St. Thérèse. Earlier in this book, we saw a doctor describe his mysterious encounter with a nun on a World War I battlefield. Possessing a "kind, gentle beauty" and "sweet face and soft features," she was tending to the dead and the dying. The doctor identified Thérèse as the nun he had met.

We also saw in the miraculous cure of a woman from County Donegal how a child was given snowdrops by a nun who was "beautiful and wore white." The child said she "had come down from on high." Having presented the flowers to her mother, she instantly recovered from her life-threatening fever and septicaemia. The family had previously been praying to Thérèse.

A further case was reported in 1910, involving a teenager from France who was dying from kidney disease and meningitis. Having been given a relic of Thérèse, he speedily recovered. "I suddenly saw before me a young nun of heavenly beauty, who looked at me with the sweetest smile," the 17-year-old reported.

"I could hear the heavenly vision saying to me: 'You will be cured,' and at the same time I was conscious of a delicious perfume, which could only have come from heaven," he later recalled. That same day, his doctor declared him to have fully recovered.

In yet another example, an apparition was reported by an 11-year-old girl who suffered from paralysis of the spinal cord. In extreme pain, she prayed to the Little Flower for a cure. One night, while in bed, she opened her eyes and saw "a pretty little face" smiling at her. "You will soon be able to walk," the apparition said. Then it vanished.

The following day, having been carried to a couch, she heard the same voice of the vision say, "Walk!" Rising to her feet, she walked for the first time in three months and threw herself into the arms of her mother. Three weeks later, she was well enough to make her First Communion. She identified the person who came to her as Thérèse, who she recognised from a picture in *Story of a Soul*.

There are many further examples of Thérèse apparitions. Although too numerous to mention, they follow a similar pattern and contain similar features, even though they come from different countries and cultures. They also stretch from shortly after the death of Thérèse right through to the story described by the two Irish women at Lourdes. In that case, but for a chance encounter, the priest's experience might never have come to light.

"I believed his story at the time, and I believe it still," Nora said, looking back. "I believe those things happen. They are not coincidences; they are God-instances. I believe St. Thérèse had come to him. Given that he was a missionary priest, and that she was the patron saint of missionaries, I think she had helped him. It was a very special thing to happen. St. Thérèse obviously had a lot of work for him to do."

Pope Francis canonised the Little Flower's parents in October 2015. Louis and Zélie Martin became the first married couple in Church history to be made saints together.

As far back as 1960, there was a flurry of activity in Ireland over the possible beatification and canonisation of the parents of Thérèse of Lisieux. Proponents of their cause took to the national press seeking public support. Readers were asked to submit petitions to Rome. To make matters easier, letters of petition could be posted to an Irish address which would further them to the Holy See.

"It is really quite easy," wrote Rev. Vernon Johnson, the convert to Catholicism who was featured earlier in this book. Having at this stage been accorded the title of monsignor, he continued: "You simply write a letter to the Holy Father petitioning him to undertake the cause of these Servants of God. Write a separate letter for each of the parents, one concerning Louis Martin and one concerning Zélie Martin. This is most important."

An address was then listed in Dublin, which would arrange for "your letter to be forwarded to His Holiness at the Vatican." Simplifying matters, a sample letter was provided, which "you should write in your own handwriting." Pointing to similar efforts being undertaken in other countries, the monsignor concluded: "The moment has come for Catholics in Ireland to join in by making their appeal."

We don't know how many newspaper readers responded to this call to arms. What we do know is that some positive force must have been at work, as, on 19 October 2008, Thérèse's parents were beatified in Lisieux and, seven years later, on 18 October 2015, they were canonised in Rome. By way of explanation regarding their elevation to sainthood, Pope Francis said they had "practiced Christian service in the family, creating day by day an environment of faith and love which nurtured the vocations of their daughters."

The canonisation was a spectacular occasion, with 65,000 people attending the Mass, including 300 cardinals, bishops and other delegates who had arrived for a synod on the family in Rome. The "family" connection was noted in remarks made by the postulator who had followed their case from start to finish. "It's the first time a couple have been canonised as a couple," he said, "and this is a beautiful sign for Christian families, who often are left without any support and have to go against the grain, especially in the west, to live and educate their children in the truth of creation and with that love that God has given us in Christ."

The miracles that led to their sainthood were equally family oriented. The first concerned an Italian child, Pietro Schilirò, who was born in May 2002 with a pulmonary malformation which left him incapable of breathing on his own. He was confined to hospital, where he was entirely dependent on artificial respiration. He lay in his bed, motionless, with his arms crossed and surrounded by a profusion of tubes.

Pietro's parents said novenas to Louis and Zélie Martin, pleading for help and praying for their beatification. At the start of their devotion, their son's health was deteriorating so rapidly that they dreaded visiting the hospital for fear of receiving bad news. One day, however, they were told on arrival of an extraordinary transformation. Not only was their son improving, but the revival was nothing short of miraculous. Within a week, he was able to breathe on his own and was soon on his way home.

The second miracle concerned a girl, Carmen Perez Pons, from Valencia, Spain. Following her mother's difficult pregnancy, she was born prematurely in 2008 and was given little chance of survival. Suffering from respiratory distress, sepsis and cerebral haemorrhaging, few believed she would live.

Her parents went to a Carmelite convent seeking help. The nuns suggested they should pray to St. Thérèse's parents, who had been beatified only days after their daughter's birth. This they did – along with family and friends – resulting in Carmen's complete recovery. There was no medical explanation for her revival.

At the conclusion of the canonisation ceremony in Rome, Pope Francis recited the Angelus in St. Peter's Square and called for the intercession of the new saints. He then suggested that families should entrust their dreams, difficulties and joys to St. Louis and St. Zélie. And so it was, on 18 October 2015 – a warm, beautiful autumn day – that the sainthood of the parents of St. Thérèse was confirmed and complete.

There is one important footnote to record. Not only were the recipients of both miracles present at the ceremony, but one of them described how – at an earlier event – he had met Pope Francis. That child was Pietro Schilirò who, although his survival was miraculous, had ended up with hearing problems. His infirmity had resulted, in March 2014, in his attendance at an audience arranged for deaf people with the pope.

Shortly before the event, his family were informed that Pope Francis would meet them personally towards its conclusion. As the pontiff walked down to the crowd, approaching those at the front, Pietro found himself stuck for words and turned to his parents asking what to say. It was too late, however, as the moment of truth had arrived.

"Pope Francis approached; he was close to me," Pietro recalled. "Mom and Dad greeted him, and Mom told him that we pray for him. Then he kissed me, and I burst into tears. I leaned against him, and my hearing aid fell to the ground. Then the pope bent down to pick it up. Dad told the pope that I was healed by a miracle granted by the Lord through the intercession of Blessed Louis and Zélie Martin, and he was very happy to hear that.

"With a big smile, he said, 'Go now, and do not cry anymore.' And with a big hug, we said goodbye to Pope Francis. Then, before waving to everyone and leaving the room, he looked at me. With his fingers he gave me the 'OK' sign. I still felt close to tears, but I was so happy because of the pope's embrace. For me, it was like meeting Jesus. I will never forget it."

ACKNOWLEDGEMENTS

Despite being a modern-day saint, biographies about St. Thérèse of Lisieux are often outdated. Many use overblown, flowery language. Others are written in a grandiose ecclesiastical style. More merely repeat stories from her memoirs. Few are easy to read. Some, however, stand out and are worth mentioning.

The best book published about Thérèse is her autobiography *Story of a Soul*. Although somewhat florid in style, it brilliantly describes her life as a child and as a nun at the Carmel in Lisieux. It also provides a comprehensive account of her little way. The book, in its numerous editions, has been translated into more than 50 languages. No matter which edition you choose, it is a fascinating read.

When writing our book, we primarily relied on Rev. T. N. Taylor's 1912 translation of *Story of a Soul*. It contains not only the saint's life story but also some of her letters, prayers and poems. A number of her miracles are also included. Taylor's edition, which sold for six shillings in 1912, was published in both Britain and America, and can be obtained with relative ease.

Another useful text was *The Life of St. Thérèse of Lisieux* by August Pierre Laveille, which was first published in English in 1929. This is the original biography commissioned by the Little Flower's sister, Mother Agnès. Although again written in an overblown fashion, the book provides a thorough background to the saint's life. *The Story of a Family* by Fr. Stéphane-Joseph Piat OFM was helpful, too. Dorothy Day's *Thérèse*, which was published in 1960, is a passionate and more modern biography, and again was of value.

Other worthwhile books which contributed to our research include Rev. William M. Cunningham's *The Unfolding of the Little Flower*, Rev. Bernard J. Quinn's *The Little Flower Booklet*, Rev. Albert H. Dolan's *Collected Little Flower Works*, Rev. Vernon Johnson's *One Lord – One Faith*, Archbishop Fulton Sheen's *St. Thérèse: A Treasured Love Story*, and *Azélie Martin: Mother of the Little Flower*, which was translated by the Earl of Wicklow. The Earl features in an excellent article by Turtle Bunbury, titled *Billy Wicklow, Ulick O'Connor and the Oxford Set*.

Many newspapers were also a rich source of information, especially *The Cork Examiner*, which later became the *Irish Examiner*, *The Irish Press*, *Irish Independent*, *Sunday Independent*, *Evening Herald*, *The Irish Times*, *Belfast Telegraph*, *Belfast News Letter* and *The Irish News and Belfast Morning News*. *The Freeman's Journal*, which folded in 1924 having been merged with the *Irish Independent*, was a further important resource, as was another defunct newspaper, Dublin's *Evening Telegraph*.

Among the religious press were the *Catholic Standard*, *Catholic Herald*, Catholic News Agency and the *Catholic Home Annual* of 1925 which featured an article, *The Little Flower*, by Cardinal Dougherty of Philadelphia. Four articles in *The Far East*, in 1934, provided invaluable insights to Thérèse's school years. The archives of the Carmel in Lisieux also contain a wealth of information and were a worthwhile resource.

Newspapers from the UK include *The Guardian* and *The Independent*. The latter contained a fine article by Spencer Leigh on Malcolm Vaughan and his controversial chart hit *St.Thérèse of the Roses*. Additional information on the singer was sourced from the American music magazine *Billboard*. *The Sevenoaks Chronicle and Kentish Advertiser* proved valuable in the Bangor, County Down, miracle featured earlier in this book. The *Campbeltown Courier* provided details on the conversion of Rev. Alexander Grant in 1911.

Some wonderful journals published at the turn of the twentieth century likewise proved of importance. *The Irish Ecclesiastical Record* – especially its August 1912 edition – was useful, as was *The Irish Rosary* and *The Catholic Bulletin*. Another journal, *Ave Maria*, published out of the USA but popular in Ireland, contained the story of French author Countess de Courson's pilgrimage to Lisieux in 1912.

We are especially grateful to Sr. Catherine Gibson of the Dominican Convent, Griffith Avenue, Dublin, for facilitating access to the 1913 edition of *The Lanthorn*. This remarkable yearbook was published by the Dominican College, Eccles Street, and contained details of an early pilgrimage to Lisieux. It was an engaging read.

For more than a century, Ireland's local newspapers have featured articles and news reports concerning the Little Flower. A search of back issues revealed additional jewels of information. We are particularly grateful to the *Munster Express, Limerick Leader, Kerryman, Sligo Champion, Connaught Telegraph, Meath Chronicle, Waterford News & Star, Dundalk Democrat, Western People, Donegal Democrat, Nenagh Guardian* and *Southern Star*.

Further insights were sourced from the *Connacht Tribune, Longford Leader, Kilkenny People, Nationalist and Leinster Times, Tuam Herald, Anglo-Celt, Drogheda Independent, Nenagh News, Leinster Express, Westmeath Examiner, Limerick Chronicle, Leitrim Observer, Donegal News* and *Connacht Sentinel*. Northern Ireland papers include the *Derry Journal, Ulster Herald, Fermanagh Herald* and *Strabane Chronicle*.

Also important were a number of local titles that are long out of business, including seven from County Kerry – the *Liberator* (Tralee), *Kerry Reporter, Kerry Advocate, Kerry Sentinel, Kerry People, Kerry News* and *Killarney Echo and South Kerry Chronicle*. There was also, of course, the famous *Skibbereen Eagle*, from County Cork, which was founded in 1857 but closed down in 1929.

Some specific titles and authors need to be thanked for their contribution to particular stories. Regarding Édith Piaf, we must single out the book *No Regrets: The Life of Édith Piaf* by Carolyn Burke, and an essay *Édith Piaf and Thérèse of Lisieux* by Fr. J. Linus Ryan, which was published at the time the film *La Vie en Rose* was released. *The Lore of Scotland: A Guide to Scottish Legends* by Jennifer Westwood and Sophia Kingshill, and *The History of Catholic Intellectual Life in Scotland 1918 – 1965* by Clifford Williamson were important sources for the 1922 Carfin Grotto story.

Of immense value regarding battlefield miracles of World War I were *Sky Pilots: The Yankee Division Chaplains in World War I* by Michael E. Shay, *Eyewitnesses to the Great War* by Ed Klekowski and Libby Klekowski, *History of the Yankee Division* by Harry A. Benwell, and *Holyoke in the Great War* by Charles S. Zack. *Storm of Glory* by John Beevers provided information relating to Zélie Martin's death.

Other specific books include *Everything is Grace* by Joseph F. Schmidt, *Making and Remaking Saints in Nineteenth-Century Britain*, edited by Gareth Atkins, *Louis and Zélie Martin* by Paulinus Redmond, *The Whole World Will Love Me* by Dorothy Scallan, *The Context of Holiness* by Marc Foley OCD, *Father William Doyle SJ* by Alfred O'Rahilly, and *To Raise the Fallen: A Selection of the War Letters, Prayers and Spiritual Writings of Fr. Willie Doyle SJ*, compiled and edited by Patrick Kenny. The latter two books were invaluable sources regarding Fr. Willie Doyle, as was the website of the Royal Dublin Fusiliers.

Another important individual you read about – Fr. Bernard J. Quinn – requires a special paragraph of his own. Among the many books we referenced were *Quintessential Priest: The Life of Father Bernard J. Quinn* by Paul W. Jervis, *Black Brooklyn: The Politics of Ethnicity, Class and Gender* by John Louis Flateau, *Love Calls: Insights of a Former Carmelite Nun* by Kimberly Braun, and the websites of both the Brooklyn Diocese of New York and St. Peter Claver Roman Catholic Church. Fr. Quinn's niece, Agnes Quinn Spalholz, wrote a letter to *The Long Island Catholic* which revealed much about his character.

Finally, on the book front, credit is due to the two volumes of *Letters of St. Thérèse of Lisieux*, translated by John Clarke OCD, *Dorothy Day and the Catholic Worker* by Nancy L. Roberts, *Firmly I Believe and Truly: The Spiritual Tradition of Catholic England*, edited by John Saward et al, and two books concerning Pope Francis – *The Great Reformer: Francis and the Making of a Radical Pope* by Austen Ivereigh and *Pope*

ACKNOWLEDGEMENTS

Francis and the Event of Encounter, edited by John C. Cavadini and Donald Wallenfang.

A number of individuals and institutions need to be thanked, including the National Library of Ireland, Cork City Library and Cork County Library. Some good friends, Jerry O'Sullivan, Weeshie Fogarty, Kathleen O'Connor, Helen Keane, and Ned and Marie Keane were always supportive. Professor Con Timon again kept the show on the road, while Linda Monahan and Barbara Ryan, of Typeform, produced their usual excellent work.

Lastly, although she is no longer with us, our thanks go to St. Thérèse of Lisieux. She taught us about the importance of little things. Her little way shows us how the trivial can become the profound; how the mundane can blossom into the rarest of flowers. In these complicated, impatient, assertive times, her message from Lisieux is appropriate and opportune.

PADRE PIO

IRISH ENCOUNTERS
WITH THE SAINT

Colm Keane

Padre Pio, the man, his miracles, priestly life, loves and hates, are described in this book. What he was like, his moods and personality, his holiness and sense of humour are featured.

You will read about his stigmata, powers of bilocation, ability to read minds, his Masses and confessions. The saint's views of women, new fashions and even his interest in football are outlined.

The man who bore the five wounds of Christ is described by those who knew, met or witnessed him.

Padre Pio: Irish Encounters with the Saint brings you up-close to an extraordinary mystic and wonderworker in a way you have never experienced before.

Reviews of *Padre Pio: Irish Encounters with the Saint*

'Fascinating book' *Belfast Telegraph*

'Couldn't put it down' *Radio Kerry*

'Reads like a thriller' *WLR Radio*

PADRE PIO

THE SCENT OF ROSES

Colm Keane

This book is crammed full of miracles and cures attributed to Ireland's favourite saint, Padre Pio, who for 50 years bore the five wounds of Christ.

Recoveries from various cancers, including tumours and leukaemia, heart problems, depression, arthritis and multiple sclerosis are recalled.

Remarkable revivals from brain injuries, infections, accidents, kidney failure, blood clots and problems in childbirth are also recounted.

Using first-hand accounts, *Padre Pio: The Scent of Roses* is written by award-winning journalist Colm Keane.

Reviews of *Padre Pio: The Scent of Roses*

'Amazing book' *Midwest Radio*

'Another page-turner' *Cork 103 FM*

'Fascinating' *Irish Independent*

THE DISTANT SHORE

MORE IRISH STORIES FROM THE EDGE OF DEATH

Colm Keane

The Distant Shore is packed with a wealth of new Irish stories about life after death.

Extraordinary accounts of what takes place when we die are featured throughout. Reunions with deceased relatives and friends, and encounters with a 'superior being', are included.

Visions of dead family members are vividly described. The book also examines astonishing premonitions of future events.

This compilation was inspired by the huge response to Colm Keane's number one bestseller Going Home – a groundbreaking book that remained a top seller for six months.

Containing new material and insights, The Distant Shore is indispensable reading for those who want to know what happens when we pass away.

Reviews of *The Distant Shore*

'Amazing new stories' *Irish Independent*

'Terrific, wonderful read' *Cork 103 FM*

'A source of genuine comfort to anyone who has suffered a bereavement' *Western People*

FOREWARNED

EXTRAORDINARY IRISH STORIES OF PREMONITIONS AND DREAMS

Colm Keane

Did you ever have a feeling that something bad was going to happen? Perhaps you dreamt of a future event? Maybe you had a 'gut feeling' that an illness, death, car crash or some other incident was about to occur?

Most Irish people, at various stages of their lives, have experienced a forewarning of the future. It may reveal itself as a sense of unease. Alternatively, it may be more intense and involve a terrifying foreboding. Perhaps it brings good news.

Forewarned is the first Irish enquiry into this intriguing phenomenon. Crammed with fascinating stories, the book also presents the latest scientific evidence proving that the future is closer to our minds than we think.

Reviews of *Forewarned*

'Amazing stories' *Belfast Telegraph*
'Authenticity of experience is written all over these reports' *The Irish Catholic*
'A fascinating read' *Soul & Spirit*

WE'LL MEET AGAIN

IRISH DEATHBED VISIONS
WHO YOU MEET WHEN YOU DIE

Colm Keane

We do not die alone. That's the remarkable conclusion of this extraordinary book examining deathbed visions.

Parents, children, brothers, sisters and close friends who have already died are among those who return to us as we pass away. Religious figures appear to others, while more see visions of beautiful landscapes.

Riveting case histories are featured, along with numerous stories from those left behind who describe after-death visitations and many other strange occurrences. The latest scientific evidence is discussed.

We'll Meet Again, written by award-winning journalist Colm Keane, is one of the most challenging books ever compiled on this intriguing theme.

Reviews of *We'll Meet Again*

'A total page-turner' *Cork 103 FM*
'Packed with riveting case histories' *LMFM Radio*
'A fascinating book' *Limerick's Live 95FM*

HEADING FOR THE LIGHT

THE 10 THINGS THAT HAPPEN
WHEN YOU DIE

Colm Keane

This explosive book reveals the truth about what happens when we die.

The ten stages we go through when we die are outlined for the very first time. They establish conclusively that death is a warm, happy experience and is nothing to fear.

Based on five years of research, the author has drawn from the real-life stories of people who have temporarily died and returned to life.

This definitive book provides you with all you need to know about the stages of death as we head for the light.

Reviews of *Heading for the Light*

'Absolutely fascinating' *RTÉ One*
'Provides much pause for thought' *Sunday Independent*
'The mysteries of dying and death from those who know'
The Irish Catholic

Capel Island Press
Baile na nGall, Ring, Dungarvan,
County Waterford, Ireland
Email: capelislandpress@hotmail.com